# The Municipal University

# THE LIBRARY OF EDUCATION

A Project of The Center for Applied Research in Education, Inc.

G. R. Gottschalk, Director

*Categories of Coverage*

| I | II | III |
|---|----|-----|
| Curriculum and Teaching | Administration, Organization, and Finance | Psychology |

| IV | V | VI |
|----|---|-----|
| History, Philosophy, and Social Foundations | Professional Skills | Educational Institutions |

# The Municipal University

WILLIAM S. CARLSON

*President*
*University of Toledo*

1962
The Center for Applied Research in Education, Inc.
*Washington, D.C.*

LIBRARY OF CONGRESS
CATALOG CARD NO.: 62–18251

PRINTED IN THE UNITED STATES OF AMERICA

60673

# Foreword

Only Dr. William S. Carlson with his unique background of experience in public higher education could have produced this interesting and stimulating treatise on *The Municipal University*. The work is at once historical, descriptive, and philosophical—answering many questions about the municipal university and bringing others into sharp focus. And the study is altogether timely, making its appearance while our rapidly changing urban civilization increases both the needs and the demands for more widespread public education among the local, state, and national communities.

The book makes it thoroughly clear that the municipal university, while sharing with its sister public and private institutions most of their responsibilities and problems, has by its nature and environment some obligations and problems that are peculiarly its own. Likewise, although its contributions and services in general are similar to those of other universities, the municipal university makes some very special additional contributions and provides some specific additional services.

The municipal university, as Dr. Carlson amply demonstrates, stands in special relation to the local tax-paying community, to the local press, to the large local alumnal constituency, and to the local political bodies. It has peculiar local admissions problems and unique responsibilities in the area of adult education. It functions under severe inhibitions where work in religion is concerned. It is automatically barred, by virtue of its tax-subsidized status, from helpful consideration by many private foundations, while being limited in the matter of public support to an amount generally far below that made available to state universities.

Insofar as the future is concerned, Dr. Carlson plainly states the dilemma created when a local community is unwilling to provide the extra tax subsidy required by the municipal university to fulfil the

v

city's own expanding educational needs and demands. Since this situation already has stimulated the search among municipal universities for county and state support, the question arises: If such support be forthcoming, will the term "municipal university" have to be redefined; indeed, will the institution, as such, disappear from the scene of United States higher education?

*The Municipal University* is an outstanding contribution to the literature of a vital national problem. Every parent, every educator, every newspaper editor, every political leader, in short, every responsible and civic-minded citizen will gain much from reading this well-written and authoritative book.

WALTER C. LANGSAM
*President*
*University of Cincinnati*

# Contents

CHAPTER I

## The Municipal University in the American Scene    1

*What Is a Municipal University?*    1
*Public and Private Education*    4
*Liberal and Vocational Education*    10
*An Educational Necessity*    12

CHAPTER II

## The Municipal University in Its Own Community    16

*Patrons and Clientele*    16
*An Investment—with Interest*    23
*Diversity in the Municipal University*    25
*Education for Democracy*    29

CHAPTER III

## Community Responsibility of the Municipal University    36

*Mutual Assistance*    36
*The Responsibility for Public Service*    42
*The Research Dilemma*    46

CHAPTER IV

## Staffing the Municipal University    52

*The Search for Faculty Members*    52

*It Takes All Kinds*                              55
*Using the City's Resources*                      57


CHAPTER   V

The Student Body of a Municipal University    62

*Environment Leaves Its Mark*                     62
*Their Educational Heritage*                      66
*To Go or Not To Go*                              68
*Religion in a Municipal University*              72


CHAPTER   VI

The Non-Degree Student                        76

*Education for the Many*                          76
*General Education*                               80
*Weighing the Programs*                           82
*Continuing Education*                            85


CHAPTER   VII

The Municipal University and the Press        88

*Spotlight on the Campus*                         88
*Reciprocal Benefits*                             91
*Joint Responsibilities*                          93


CHAPTER   VIII

The Future of the Municipal University        97

Bibliography                                 101

Index                                        105

*The Municipal University*

CHAPTER I

# The Municipal University
# in the American Scene

If we are an ignorant people, we must suffer limitations upon our freedom or be governed by ignorance. If we are an enlightened people, our government of ourselves will be enlightened . . . Insofar as education is available to us and effective, we may hope as a nation to govern ourselves with justice and magnanimity, to the benefit of ourselves and to the benefit of the world. Insofar as the local public college makes such education available to more and more people it is democracy's college.[1]

## What Is a Municipal University?

Municipal universities make up a small segment of higher education, a few institutions among the many in the more general categories. Even trying to make an exact count is difficult, for the number varies somewhat depending upon the interpretation of the definition used. A practical definition, however, might be that a municipal university is an institution of higher learning supported in part by local taxation and administered by a local governing board to bring the services of higher education to the community.

A municipal university is classified as a "publicly controlled" institution because a majority of the members of the governing board obtain their appointments through an action by a governmental agency of the municipality in which the university is located. Perhaps equally important with the selection of the members of the governing board is the fact that board members are residents of the community, living near the university and meeting frequently. In one instance they are elected by the board of education; in another, eight are appointed by the governor and two are ex officio, the governor and the mayor. In two cities, four members are appointed by the board of education, four by the city commission, and

[1] John S. Diekhoff, *Democracy's College* (New York: Harper & Brothers, 1950), p. 201.

1

the ninth member is the mayor, ex officio. In all other instances the appointments are by the mayor, usually with approval of the council or aldermen.

With one exception the boards which control municipal universities are small, not exceeding nine or ten members, with terms ranging from four to ten years. The exception is the Board of Higher Education of New York City, whose twenty-one members (plus one ex officio) govern four large degree-granting institutions and three two-year community colleges.

Note that the term "university" indicates a degree-granting program; junior colleges and community colleges are not included in the roster of municipal universities, although the two-year institutions are supported by local taxes and are administered by boards representing the citizens of the community. As in any institution bearing the name "university," it is ordinarily expected that a municipal university will maintain a program of graduate studies and a number of professional schools, as well as a strong core of the liberal arts. Single-purpose colleges with degree-granting programs, such as the few municipal teachers colleges that still exist, are normally not included in the definition of "municipal university," although an engineering college is listed in this category, but with some reservations.

Support in part by local taxation is part of the definition. Tax money may make up any proportion of operating funds, from a small percentage to more than half. Local tax income may be derived by a number of different methods· of taxation and may involve a direct vote of the citizens or allocation by a legislative body of the city. The term "local taxation" does not exclude additional funds from other sources, although a negligible or token contribution from local taxes would hardly qualify an institution to label itself municipal. The term "municipal" seems to be avoided in formal names, the Municipal University of Omaha being the only one in which the word actually occurs.

The Education Directory 1960–61 of the U.S. Department of Health, Education and Welfare lists 314 institutions as under district or city control. This indicates that 15.4 per cent of the 2,028 institutions of higher education in the nation receive some local support. It represents a net increase of about 50 institutions during the last ten years, which can be attributed primarily to community colleges offering two-year programs.

While only a scattered dozen of the 314 meet the requirements to be included among municipal universities, it would be misleading to brush these off as an unimportant segment of higher education. They represent an interesting development in American democracy and they continue to fill an important need in heavily populated areas. In the fall of 1961 they enrolled 140,045 students. Of these, 81,798 or 58 per cent were attending Brooklyn College, City College, Hunter College, and Queens College, which are operated by the Board of Higher Education of New York City and are all included under the legal title of the City University of New York.[2]

Other institutions which meet the terms of the definition are, according to the 1961 fall registrations, the University of Cincinnati, 18,638; Municipal University of Omaha, 7,287; The University of Toledo, 6,963; University of Louisville, 5,983; University of Akron, 6,376; University of Wichita, 5,748; Washburn University of Topeka, 3,408; and Newark College of Engineering, 3,824.[3] Louisville's status is not as clear-cut as the rest, for it identifies itself as a private university with municipal support. This support, however, is sizable: its board is approved by the city aldermen, and city residents enjoy the advantage of lower fees. Both Louisville and the Newark College of Engineering receive substantial amounts from the state, although in the former case the money is earmarked for the medical school only. The Newark College of Engineering is of interest because half its income was from state appropriations and only five per cent from city funds in 1962–63. President Van Houten notes that Newark College of Engineering has been called "an instrumentality of the state," and that the college is not a

---

[2] Garland G. Parker, "Statistics of Attendance in American Universities and Colleges, 1961–1962," *School and Society*, January 13, 1962.

[3] These figures are used because they are assembled at about the same time and the method of counting has some uniformity. However, as an example of the variations one may encounter, the City University of New York, which was credited with 77,621 in the *School and Society* issue of Jan. 14, 1961, listed its total enrollments for fall, 1960, as 87,322 in the four colleges. Of these 31,751 were full time and 55,571 were part time. (From a folder, "The City University of New York" dated April 15, 1961.) Reports from the other universities would show similar differences between early fall figures and those compiled later in the year.

municipal institution in the same sense as the three in Ohio.[4] The state of New York provides full support for teacher education in the City University of New York.

As might be expected, only a city of fairly large population can afford to maintain a municipal university. In the existing group of such institutions in the United States, Washburn University at Topeka, Kansas, is the only one located in a city of less than 250,000 population (1960 census).

Among the municipal universities as listed for some years, three are now missing. The College of Charleston, South Carolina, smallest of the group and first (1837) to have municipal support, has reverted to private control, which was its original status. Wayne University in Detroit, Michigan, one of the largest, has become a full state university. Midwestern University of Wichita Falls, Texas, which evolved from a municipal junior college into a four-year municipal institution in 1946 and received its present name in 1950, was transferred from municipal to full state support on September 1, 1961.

A discussion of municipal universities limits itself first to the few four-year institutions which receive tax support from the local community and which are governed by a board representing the citizens of the community. Consideration of the problems of this group involves many matters of equal concern to all universities that carry on their work in a large city environment. The problems in many cases transcend the form of support or geographical location to become the concerns of higher education as a whole.

## Public and Private Education

Unity of purpose is one of the keystones which those in higher education have retained while introducing a great many divergent modes. The interests shared by America's colleges and universities, whether public or private, are much greater than their differences. Any discussion of municipal universities is certain to be a commentary on all institutions of higher education with only minor differences, created principally by the method of support and the local nature of control.

---

[4] Robert W. Van Houten, letter to the author, March 7, 1962.

What are the respective purposes of the different types of institutions of higher learning? Can a definition of purposes be drawn so as to exclude either public or privately controlled education? From reading a statement of institutional purposes, can one distinguish between state universities and municipal universities, between privately controlled urban institutions and those supported by taxes?

The more one gets back to fundamentals, even though seeming to verge on the impossibly trite, the more the essential unity of American higher education will be realized. If the function of higher education is reduced to the basic purpose of producing citizens capable of supporting themselves, of contributing to the welfare of others, of making wise decisions, of furthering knowledge—institutions of all classifications are one and alike. Higher education cannot share such a great goal without conceding that the interests of all who are engaged in it are held in common. All have historic bases offering adequate explanation for the divergent paths which various colleges and universities choose for accomplishing the same end.

In colonial times and even later, the primary role of higher education was the preparation of ministers. It is the changing pattern and temper of the American people themselves which have brought about the development of the present system of higher education. The population, its needs and its aspirations, seem far removed today from the days of the schools founded by the ardent alumni of the great pioneering colleges of New England. The state and municipal universities, when they came along later, did not arrive in a vacuum. They were created by the citizenry in response to widely felt demands. The privately operated colleges and universities first on the scene claimed the geographic and curricular areas in which they would operate, and the needs which they could not meet had to be faced by the public.

Furthermore, limitations of transportation during the nineteenth and early twentieth centuries made it necessary for the college student to live on or near the campus. With improved highways, more automobiles, and rapid transit systems more students were able to commute daily from greater distances and thereby save the additional cost of living away from home. While the better-known prestige universities continued to draw the majority of their students from a wide area, other institutions found their clientele coming increasingly from within commuting distance. As cities and complex metropolitan areas grew in America, the institution most accessible to the greatest number of students was the one located at or near home. Thus, there developed institutions of higher education with the distinctive characteristic of serving students primarily located within areas having well-developed transportation. In recent years, however, these institutions have drawn students from a wider area and have long since ceased to be purely local or municipal in nature.

The state of Ohio, for example, has a cluster of three strong municipal universities. They operate under a state law of 1870 and are supported by local taxation, gifts, fees, and local appropriations. Up to the present, no state financial aid has been granted these institutions, although it has been discussed frequently in each city and bills toward this end have been introduced during the last several sessions of the Legislature. The University of Cincinnati, founded in 1819, has had municipal support since 1870; The University of Akron, founded in 1870, since 1913, and The University of Toledo, founded in 1872, since 1884. Thus, for 216 of their 322 years, support of these universities has been the responsibility of their respective cities. Once almost entirely local, they now show the trends outlined earlier in this chapter. Currently, students from 81 of Ohio's 88 counties attend the University of Cincinnati. Forty-four counties are represented at The University of Toledo and 30 at the University of Akron.

These three, plus five state universities and one state college make up the publicly supported institutions of higher education in Ohio. In the three cities, which have about one tenth of the state's population, the municipal universities enroll nearly 30 per cent of the students in all the state's tax supported institutions. Taking into account Ohio's 39 private colleges and universities, the three municipal universities enroll about 18 per cent of all the college students in the state.[5] Thus, with local support, the municipal universities in Ohio have shouldered an ever-growing share of the responsibility for higher education. This has not been easy, for

---

[5] "State Supported Higher Education in 1961," *Operation and Financing of State Programs* (Ohio). Published by the Governor's Office, 1962.

over the years it has been necessary for their communities to assist these institutions in building up physical plants valued at some $90 million. As Chancellor Heald has put it:

. . . urban institutions are located in cities where most of the students live at home and commute to classes. The direct service of these institutions to their communities and to society in general is their hallmark. More than any other force in America, they have brought education to the people . . . The rise and growth of the urban institution in the past quarter of a century has been phenomenal. Urban institutions have broadened the base of higher education and helped make the democratic dream come true for thousands of youth.[6]

The Association of Urban Universities estimates that there are about 200 big city colleges and universities in the United States. These represent one tenth of all the institutions of higher education in the United States, but they enroll more than half the entire college population of the country.[7]

It is much easier to identify principal types of eminent and metropolitan universities than to categorize individual institutions. Most universities, on the one hand, have aspirations for national prominence and can point to features of their programs that indicate progress in this direction. On the other hand, distinguished universities cannot avoid responding to features and needs in their local environments. All urban universities have many characteristics in common, as indicated by the existence and activities of the Association of Urban Universities, which includes both the most and the least prominent metropolitan institutions in its membership.

In general, the metropolitan university in America is either privately or municipally controlled and financed, for with notable exceptions, state colleges and universities have been located away from large urban centers. In Ohio four of the five state universities are in small communities. The Ohio State University is in Columbus, the state capital, a city somewhat smaller in population than Cincinnati. In Michigan neither the University of Michigan nor Michigan State University are in the Detroit urban area. A similar

---

[6] From an address by Chancellor Henry T. Heald, New York University, at the inauguration of Francis H. Horn as the President of Pratt Institute, May 15, 1954.

[7] Ruth Weinstock, *Space and Dollars: An Urban University Expands* (New York: Educational Facilities Laboratories, 1961), p. 7.

situation exists in many other states which have large urban areas—for example, Illinois, Iowa, Indiana, Wisconsin, and Texas—although in some of these, branches of the state university are maintained in the largest metropolitan area in the state. Minnesota is a notable exception with its state university located in Minneapolis.

In some large cities both municipal and privately controlled universities have grown side by side. In Detroit, for instance, there is Wayne State University, formerly a municipal institution, and the University of Detroit which is privately controlled; in Cincinnati, the University of Cincinnati and Xavier University. In cities the size of Toledo there is more likely to be either a municipal university or one that is privately controlled, but hardly both, unless the latter is limited to a certain kind of student or to only a few programs.

As was the case in Ohio, a struggling private institution may be taken over by the city in order to enable it to serve the community better. The trend now is toward state rather than municipal support in such instances. The University of Buffalo has long been privately controlled but has repeatedly conducted fund raising drives in the community. In 1961 it changed its status to public control as a unit of the State University of New York. The University of Houston, once private, also became state supported in 1961.

The needs for publicly supported higher education have increased and will continue to do so. The present and projected population trend is toward urbanization of the nation's population, which means that in the future a greater proportion of young people seeking higher education will come from the urban centers. The total of high school graduates will be on a sharply ascending curve in the foreseeable future. A more complex world and, indeed, national survival, require increasing numbers of men and women qualified for leadership, and the pressure will be upon the tax-supported institutions to expand their facilities.

The general philosophy of education that pervades the operation of a municipal university goes far beyond the accepted philosophy of the traditional university of several decades ago. Just as the public high schools with their differentiated curriculums have come to fulfill a needed function quite different from that of the classical private academy of the last century, so the modern municipal university is helping to show how to adapt higher education to the needs of a greater segment of the people in the community. Discussion and debate are generated by topics such as the place of the liberal arts, professional programs, technical education, adult education, graduate programs, community service, basic and/or applied research, short courses, off-campus programs, contract programs, evening courses, part-time instructors, televised courses, and intercollegiate athletics.

The traditional college of the past served a select few, chosen carefully on the basis of scholarship and probably other considerations not too democratic, such as family position and wealth. It set up its own curricular standards in terms of time-honored classical education. The standards of achievement it required were in terms of the student's ability to master a set of traditional subject matter. In contrast, the municipal college, by its very nature, cannot be arbitrarily selective in the long-accepted sense. Its function is not to serve a few at the expense of many, but rather to study the community to learn how, where, and to whom it can be of greatest service in the field of higher education. It must shape its program to meet educational needs of many different types.

The municipal university cannot, in all fairness, claim that it has been the leader in effecting modern trends in higher education. Perhaps it would be better to say that municipal universities, because of their location in population centers, have been required to meet the needs revealed by social changes and consequent changes in educational thinking. Municipal universities, like all universities, need to examine most carefully the demands which society makes upon education and to determine which of these demands have a genuine and continuing validity. Only on such a foundation will the municipal universities progress. The American people in their concern for material values are making increasing demands, as they have for many years past, for vocational and professional preparation in school, college, and university. This applies particularly to municipal universities because of the nature of their student bodies. Most municipal universities and some other institutions of higher learning have sought to fill the demand. Still others, although reluctant, have been unable to resist the pressure. In consequence, during recent years more emphasis has been placed on professional or vocational education than on liberal arts education.

The trend is present and real. It needs to be assessed by the municipal universities with care, lest over the years higher education produces men and women who can act skillfully but who cannot think, people who are trained but not civilized, people who are deaf and blind in the arts, and because of their ignorance of history, know nothing of the values of tradition and who exist only in the present with no sense of continuity.

Professional education is attractive because it has relevance to immediate demands. The modern economy clamors for graduates "practically" trained. Conformity to the value of practicality seems to be the twentieth century ideal in many institutions, and it is obvious that present conditions will not moderate the pressure for professional and vocational training. No prophet is needed to predict that universities and colleges will be expected to provide more practical curriculums.

### Liberal and Vocational Education

Educators in municipal universities are constantly raising the question of whether their institutions can be liberal and vocational at the same time. The answer, invariably, is "yes." Are these areas mutually exclusive? Must a municipal university sacrifice the arts in order to do a good job of training? Municipal university educators think not. As educators they recognize the leavening and enriching values of liberal arts and believe that universities are experiencing a shift in emphasis rather than a cancellation of the enduring worth of the liberal disciplines.

In the nineteenth century people knew what was meant when a man was referred to as "educated." Today the definition is confused, and two schools of thought are so scornful of each other that they sometimes are blind to the possibilities of the intermingling of vocational and liberal disciplines. In actual practice more and more emphasis is placed on the general or "liberal" educational offering within vocational curriculums. The educator in a municipal university sees no cogent reason to assume that an engineer must be only a partially educated man.

The most common misconception of a university is that it is a collection of professional schools, but this belies both tradition and the name itself. Professional schools are concerned with the application of a body of knowledge to specialized problems. The importance of their role in modern society is too generally recognized to require comment. But professional schools alone do not make a university; they are properly found in the context of a university. They benefit greatly from the association, as the university benefits from their presence. Their operation is enhanced in many ways by the association of faculty and students with those who are engaged in extending the boundaries of human knowledge, as the latter may profit by seeing the consequences of their discoveries in the work of the former.

A university is an organization of men and women associated solely for the purpose of discovering and disseminating knowledge. A university must seek general knowledge; its concern must be comprehensive; it must seek knowledge for its own sake in the natural sciences, the social sciences, and the humanities, and in all departments of each of these. In its concern with dissemination as well as discovery, it must begin with the thirteenth grade and continue to the doctoral dissertation and beyond. In its inquiries, it is motivated chiefly by the innate desire of the human spirit to know. Experience reveals that nothing else—not even vocational aims—motivates as effectively as this high purpose. The knowledge thus achieved justifies itself and all else depends on it. A university, in this sense, is the keystone of educational enterprises.

The definition of a university in terms of the search for knowledge for its own sake is sometimes considered too narrow. Some would say that university education is for democracy, for citizenship, for the whole man, for adaptation to one's environment, or for effective group living. There is a serious error implicit in such a formulation, although a university may have these and other attendant values. Men can be educated for democracy in various ways and through various agencies; but the university cannot, without distortion, become an agency designed for indoctrination, no matter how great or good the cause. A university is a body of teachers and students committed to the intrinsic value of knowledge. That this is the function which identifies the university is well stated in "Academic Freedom in our Time," a study prepared for the Academic Freedom Project by Robert M. MacIver of Columbia University:

> If the university makes the inculcation of this virtue (of seeking the truth) its special concern, it will at once be true to itself and make its best contribution to the moral life of the community.

## An Educational Necessity

The urgent need in most municipalities for a university which truly fulfills these lofty objectives is apparent on a number of grounds:

1. There is a fundamental obligation in a democratic society for the city or state, as the case may be, to provide for equality among its citizens. Economic equality does not require that all men have equal possessions or equal incomes, but rather that they all have an opportunity to work, at least a minimum subsistence, and compensation commensurate with the productivity of their work. Social equality does not require that all men have the same education, but it does require that their education be limited only by their ability and their interests. An educational program for a free people must concentrate on developing the power of critical judgment within individual citizens, not on indoctrination and inculcation of attitudes. A program designed to develop the students' critical faculties and analytical powers is characteristic of a good university.

A responsible city or state cannot rely on fortuitous circumstances for the education of its citizens. Only the existence of public low-cost higher education can insure that each youth will be able to develop his individual potentialities, now and in the future. Government cannot influence, much less control, private institutions in order to satisfy its obligations in higher education. Since the Dartmouth College case of 1819, which proved the freedom of private institutions, it has been clear that a state can control educational policies, standards of admission, and so forth in state-operated institutions only. Inasmuch as the state has an obligation in the field of higher education—and ultimately this obligation can be no less than it is in primary and secondary education—then there must be public higher education institutions that are comprehensive and adequate.

2. That there is this inescapable public responsibility for higher education has been generally asserted both in ancient times and today. This responsibility was commonplace for the Greeks. As Aristotle says in his *Politics:*

> No one will doubt that the legislator should direct his attention above all to the education of youth; for the neglect of education does harm to the state.

The Council of State Governments, in a contemporary statement, says:

> State-supported higher education fulfills important functions in making education of high quality available at relatively low cost to individuals, and in helping to provide educational opportunities to young people even though they may not have demonstrated clearly superior intellectual capacities in high school. These special features of public institutions need to be preserved.

In this statement the Council also calls attention to the important safety-valve function of a public institution: Slow starters may find increasing difficulty in gaining entrance to private institutions, but tragic injustice may result from their total exclusion.

The significance of public higher education to the city or state is eloquently recognized by a California restudy of the needs in higher education:

> From the colonial beginnings of the United States, farsighted citizens and responsible statesmen have recognized that the safety, the welfare, and the happiness of our people must depend in large part upon the fullest possible understanding of nature and of man and his needs. To promote and to disseminate such understanding, and also to give it scope and application, most states have established universities dedicated to scientific and scholarly research, to teaching the ablest of their youth, to training them for careers in the professions, and to carrying out investigations of fundamental and practical problems in agriculture, engineering, medicine, commerce, public health, public administration, education, and other fields.

3. Research is another great area in which a municipal university can make a unique contribution. The vitality, security, and welfare of a people might well be measured in terms of the research activi-

ties in which it engages. The benefits which society has received from university research defy description. Although all effects of research may not have a positive benefit, very frequently the results of research are of such tremendous consequence that no state can afford to leave its prosecution to chance, to the gifts of philanthropy, to the needs of national defense, or to the limited objectives of industry. The public must assume responsibility for insuring a comprehensive program of basic research. Since the public cannot and should not do this by subsidizing, hence controlling the research programs of private institutions, it must establish and equip its own institutions where inquiry may proceed, directed only by the insights and curiosity of the competent inquiring mind. According to the California restudy, the fundamental justification for research lies in sheer human curiosity, in the need and hunger to understand. When this hunger is frustrated:

> . . . human personality tends to deteriorate—men tend to be more distracted by confusion, suspicion, anxiety and fear, and more vulnerable to domination by brutal and tyrannical forces; whereas, where inquiry is vigorous and free there is a better chance for men to achieve independence and self respect and the satisfaction of realizing their capacities.

4. The need of urban centers for the kind of university which was described above becomes apparent when one considers the probable consequences of the failure to provide for it. As the number of students demanding admission to educational institutions increases, more and more of them will be forced to turn to the public institutions because of insufficient privately operated facilities. Because of their obligation, public institutions may find it necessary to turn away some qualified applicants for lack of facilities.

5. All statistics clearly forecast a tremendous increase in college population by 1970. Many private colleges and universities, on the one hand, have a tradition to uphold inconsistent with such expansion; moreover, being privately endowed and controlled, they are under no moral obligation to make any changes which deviate from the purposes for which they were established. A public institution, on the other hand, must be responsive to the needs of large numbers for higher education.

It is the obligation of a municipal university to lead. A society which formulates its programs by consulting the passions of its adolescents rather than the wisdom of some of its most intelligent citizens is inviting disaster. What people want is determined to a considerable extent by what is presented to them. A citizen ought to be able to have a well-founded faith in the ability of his public university to provide his children with the education which they should have. An education program should not be determined simply by the desires of its prospective students or by the demands of industry. Enlightened leaders of industry are becoming progressively aware of this. It is the job of an educator to discover the nature and function of a university. In the true university is found a group of educators, not simply a single educator in isolation.

# CHAPTER II

# The Municipal University in Its Own Community

. . . It is generally known that many of these [municipal] institutions were founded through private grants of money, land and buildings by well-to-do citizens of the city. As time went on, and these private resources proved to be inadequate to meet the rapidly growing public demand for their academic and professional services, most cities had to give serious thought to the granting of tax or other public support to the university, college, or institute. As a consequence there have developed many different kinds and combinations of private and public support and control of these urban institutions. Some have essentially private boards of control and consider themselves different than public universities. Others have, in whole or in part, publicly elected or appointed boards and think of themselves as essentially municipal or public institutions. In varying degrees all of these universities grew in public favor as well as in size and variety of offerings because they brought their academic, professional, and technical programs to the community in which they were established.[1]

## Patrons and Clientele

Of the major characteristics of higher education, none is more vital than that it remains independent, noncommercial, and nonpolitical. While research and training may be pursued with the active collaboration of industry or government and while funds may come from political and business sources, the tradition of academic freedom still flourishes in institutions of higher education. An important element of this freedom is the right to determine educational objectives without outside pressures. Experience of some of the municipal universities is shown in their answers to direct questions

[1] Winfred A. Harbison, "Bringing the Resources of the University to the Community Through Academic Offerings." A paper at the conference on The Role of the University in an Urban Setting, the University of Wisconsin-Milwaukee, October 28, 1960.

such as: To what extent are you free to select your objectives? Are there pressure groups in your community that attempt to exercise control over your budget or your curriculum? These appear in an informal questionnaire sent by the author to presidents of municipal universities in the spring of 1961. University officials in these municipal institutions indicate they feel they have the confidence of community groups. Suggestions are not unusual, but organized attempts to exert pressure are rare. This is a good sign, indicating that the board, administration, and faculty are considered able to make sound professional judgments about higher education. Probably it indicates, too, that they make it their responsibility to be aware of the community and its peculiar needs.

But to continue as an institution controlled by objectives determined by itself rather than by others, the university must have adequate financial support, which is not restricted to particular activities or derived from the sale of services. It must have patrons. The patron is the person, organization, or agency which provides financial support without strings attached, and without demanding control over the university.

A university must also have an interested and active clientele if it is to survive. The clientele of a municipal university includes the members of the university's board of control, the individuals, institutions, and agencies who are patrons, those interested in research results, the parents of students, interested employers of students, graduates, and the students themselves. Higher education must have support from its customers. In the municipal universities the local taxpayer is the most important supporter. His patronage is made effective through the local governing body. In general this local support comes through direct appropriations, separate tax levies, or both.

Considered in relation to the total income from all tax sources and student fees, these local tax funds vary in amount from less than 6 per cent at the Newark College of Engineering to nearly 50 per cent at the Universities of Akron and Wichita and slightly more than 50 per cent at Washburn University of Topeka. Most of the rest are in the 40 per cent bracket, the exceptions being the Universities of Cincinnati (32 per cent) and Louisville (22 per cent). In the last two mentioned a medical school may be the main factor affecting the percentage.[2]

In six of the universities, students pay more than half of the total which comes from public funds and student fees combined. At Akron the percentage is 50.3; at Wichita, 51.0; at Toledo, 57.7; at Omaha, 59.8; at Cincinnati, 66.5 and at Louisville, 76.9. The four senior colleges in the City University of New York receive only 16.2 per cent of the total from the students, while at Newark it is 41 per per cent and at Washburn University of Topeka it is 42 per cent.

City funds in New York, amounting to more than $22,000,000 for the four senior colleges, are made available through a budget adopted by the City Board of Estimate and the City Council. The Board of Higher Education finds that operating allocations on a line basis are somewhat restrictive and it is seeking power to make its own changes within lump sum appropriations.

An annual appropriation by the Board of Aldermen provides city funds in Louisville following a budget hearing before the mayor and other officials. Of the city appropriation of a little more than a million dollars in 1960–61, the sum of $125,000 was earmarked for the medical school. In Newark requests go to the mayor and to the City Council for a direct appropriation.

Six of the universities receive funds from a tax millage. The city charters of Akron, Cincinnati, and Toledo contain such provisions as the result of popular vote. The levy in each case is two mills, the second mill being voted for Cincinnati in 1962. Toledo receives no other local tax money except as it may be allocated by the Council for capital improvements from time to time. Akron has a 0.45-mill levy for capital improvements voted for five years, and also an annual appropriation from the City Council. Such appropriations are not obligatory. In Omaha the university receives funds from a mill levy against both real and personal property in the city. Changes in millage are possible when authorized by the State Legislature to go on the local ballot and then approved by ma-

---

[2] Round figures and percentages used in this and the following section are based on 1960–61 financial reports of the institutions mentioned and correspondence between officials of these universities and the author. They are an attempt to draw pictures which might be relatively comparable for more than a single year. This is the reason for using the income from student fees and public funds rather than total income from all sources in making the comparisons.

jority vote of the citizens of Omaha. The tax situation at Washburn University of Topeka and the University of Wichita is unusual in that the Board of Regents in each instance levies its own taxes within the statutory authority of five mills (including sales tax residue) for operating and 1.25 mills for debt retirement and construction. The proposed budget and tax levy must be advertised for public hearing before adoption.

City governments in most cases are not averse to distributing the educational burden over a wide base. County or district support is one solution. Partial state support for special programs—teacher education, medicine, engineering, community or junior college—has come to the aid of the limited resources of the city in several instances. The Newark College of Engineering, for example, is quite unlike the rest in that something more than half of all its revenue is state money. This is appropriated by the Legislature after approval of the budget by the State Board of Education and recommendation of the Governor. The money, 1.8 million dollars in 1960–61, is made available as a contract arrangement for the purchase of higher educational opportunities in the field of engineering for New Jersey residents. A half million annually is appropriated by the State of Kentucky for the medical school at the University of Louisville. At Cincinnati, however, the medical college receives no state funds.

The two municipal universities in Kansas for the first time in 1961–62 received state money through an appropriation by the Legislature in the amount of $3.00 a credit hour for all work within the first 60 credit hours taken by residents of Kansas. The state supplies a substantial amount for the City University of New York, totaling nearly $20,000,000 or about 39 per cent of all public funds and student fees. These state funds, as a result of legislation enacted in 1959 and in 1960, are intended to provide for the entire cost of teacher education and one third the cost of the first two years of the colleges. The Municipal University of Omaha and the three Ohio institutions receive no state aid. The University of Cincinnati, however, does receive about $30,000 and the University of Toledo about $15,000 for conducting vocational educational programs for the state.

Two institutions have received support from nearby political areas. At Louisville, in the academic year 1961–62, Jefferson County made an appropriation to equalize tuition rates between city residents and those living in the county outside the city limits. This amounts to more than a half million dollars a year. In 1960 voters of Golf Manor, Ohio, a suburb of Cincinnati, approved a two-mill property tax levy for five years for the benefit of the University of Cincinnati. Under this arrangement students from this area will pay the same fees as residents of the city proper.

Basically the municipal universities have two principal sources of funds: public monies and student fees. Large endowments are not characteristic of municipal universities, the income from this source being most sizable at those with the medical schools. In 1960–61 the University of Cincinnati had by far the largest return from endowments, $897,000; the University of Louisville was the only other with more than $200,000 for the year, and of all the rest only Washburn University received more than $100,000. Some funds are available from research, gifts, and other sources; but these do not make up more than a small percentage of the total except, again, where medical schools are involved. The University of Cincinnati reported more than $4,000,000 and the University of Louisville more than $3,000,000 for the year.

Student fees may be broken down into tuition, laboratory, and services, the last including such categories as student activities, health, classroom materials, parking, student union, and so forth. In some cases tuition itself may be free to residents of the area which provides the tax support. A statement for the City University of New York reads:

> Tuition for baccalaureate degree programs is free for qualified residents of the city and for qualified residents of the state who are preparing to teach . . . New York State students not preparing to teach may enroll for baccalaureate study, paying tuition of $350 a year. Tuition fees are paid by all other students in undergraduate, graduate, and adult education courses . . . Laboratory and service fees are paid by all students.

Most municipal universities see themselves in an area somewhere between state-supported and private institutions. Fees for non-residents, for example, may be nearly as high as those in some of the privately controlled colleges and universities. In return for local support, the resident of the city enjoys lower fees, but these often are higher than charges in state universities. Low tuition fees are sharply restricted to those whose homes are within the corporate boundaries of the municipality. In Toledo, for example, a student who lives only two blocks west of the campus is outside the city limits and can attend a state university 20 miles away more cheaply than the municipal University of Toledo, which he can see from his own front yard.

Theoretically the difference between resident and nonresident fees should represent the per student or per credit hour value of the city's contribution. In other words it is a subvention to each resident student. In practice the calculation is not so simple. For example, in two municipal universities of nearly equal size, budget and city support, undergraduate fees for out-of-town students at one are double those for residents while at the other they are only one third higher. In a third, somewhat smaller school, the difference is but one dollar a credit hour. Perhaps the difference depends on what the traffic will bear in relation to whether the institution wishes to attract out-of-town students.

Because of the possibility of state aid for more of the municipal institutions, a three-level fee system may become common. This would mean one set of charges for students from the city or district, a second for other residents of the state, and a third, highest of all, for students who come from outside the state.

When students enter the ranks of the alumni, they become automatically another important segment of the supporting clientele of the municipal institution. The questionnaire mentioned earlier indicates that alumni interest is on the increase, but in terms of dollars and cents their efforts fall far short of the assistance which many private and a few state institutions receive from their graduates.

The alumnus who remains in his home city commonly brings up the fact that as a taxpayer he continues to help support his alma mater and this should relieve him of any further financial obligation. Spoken or unspoken, this may be the major reason for a low rate of alumni giving both in amounts and in percentage of participation. A little arithmetic shows that in Cincinnati taxes toward university support amount to roughly $6.00 per capita annually, and in Toledo less than $5.50—hardly a back-breaking burden.

But these comments are not to belittle the value of the local alumni. Strategically they are of tremendous importance, bunched in large numbers where community interest is most needed by the institution. Municipal university presidents report that alumni have been especially helpful in campaigns in which tax issues or other university matters were at stake. Alumni can and do rally to specific situations. Often this support has been excellent where the objective is concrete; a building, for example. It is unfortunate that alumni are not stirred to action as easily when funds are needed for faculty salaries. The more thoughtful attention being given by these institutions to alumni interests may help overcome this situation in the future.

A distinction should be made between the motives or interests of those who become part of a municipal university's supporting clientele. At one extreme is the no-strings-attached philanthropic interest, and at the other is the business interest. Somewhere in between is the investment type of interest, usually represented by the taxpayer or the industry that is looking for a long term gain. The alumnus may be in any one of the categories.

A philanthropist's interest is based upon the value to society of independent and free higher education, upon the value of having the institution pursue its own ends according to its own judgment. An investment type interest is based upon the university incorporating objectives which are of importance to the party providing support. Such an objective could be, for instance, research or the training of teachers, pharmacists, or nurses. The person with a business-type interest turns to the university only because it happens to offer the cheapest way for him to satisfy a particular need, not because of any belief in the value of independent higher education. He becomes a customer of the university just as he would become a customer of any commercial organization.

Parents and students have a wide variety of motives which bring them into the municipal university. Not enough of them feel that the liberal education provided by a university is of importance to an individual and society. The great majority turn to the university as the most readily available place for the purchase of training in specific skills leading to a vocation or profession. The cultivation of these patrons must be emphasized because their support is vital to the continued growth of municipal universities. Student fees, which have increased in amount, are of importance to institutions as more and more students are enrolled, and the prospects are for even higher enrollments. These students also are taxpayers or potential taxpayers. Likewise, sponsored research has become prominent in the financial affairs of municipal universities. So, in recent years the number of customers of higher education have been increasing faster than the number of sponsors.

## An Investment—with Interest

If one's interest is where he puts his money, then the taxpayers have a right to pay some attention to their municipal university. They are somewhat akin to stockholders in the institution; they can be a help or a hindrance, sometimes simultaneously. It comes as a shock, however, to find at times how little information many of them really do have about the institution, and it is even more of a jolt to discover how many of them do not care. This is a situation known to all who take an interest in public relations.

The educator, on the one hand, gets so wrapped up in his own work that it is hard for him to realize that there are many who pay no attention at all. On the other hand, every university has many friends, some quite vocal, who *do* pay attention to what goes on. These should be reached with factual information so that their attitudes will be based on more than half-truths, hearsay, and emotion. Where the constituency is so close at hand, as in the municipal university, the institution should try to make the very best of the situation.

University officials tread a dangerous path if they believe that a flow of communication can make everyone like and appreciate the university. Perhaps in some cases, if people who seem unfriendly were able to get all the facts, this attitude might turn into something much worse. Public attitudes about an institution are based on what it really is, not what it says it is. In an urban environment it is difficult for an institution to fool many people for very long about its true character. Thus, the administration and board of the municipal university find themselves under a strong light. They are watched; they are given suggestions and criticism; their performance is scrutinized by many who take more than a passing interest.

The board members and the president are in a sense public servants; yet their responsibility is for educational leadership, which may, at times, require considerable diplomacy. They cannot acquiesce to every suggestion or demand from some part of the public. They may have to make decisions which can be unpopular, such as raising student fees. Nor does general public acclaim follow a decision to seek an increase in support through added taxes. These steps, however, may at times be necessary to maintain and improve an academic institution.

University officials base their appeal for public support and appreciation on "the value of the university to the community" or "education as a community investment." They ask for funds and friends and in return they promise, explicitly or implicitly, certain services. These services should result in a better community—culturally, economically, or politically—preferably all three. How successfully the university can produce, as well as promise, depends not only upon faculty and facilities but upon the spirit in which it carries out its work.

It is not easy to determine what the community expects from its university—what it desires it to be and do. Nor is it easy to say what the various interests of the public—business, industry, the professions, special interest groups, and so forth—should have from it. By what means is this to be determined? How will the value of judgments on such matters be tested? How much dependence can be placed on so-called experts who view the academic scene on a broader scale, but who hardly can be fully aware of the intricate relationships of one particular institution? Or are there overriding factors which hold true regardless of time, place, or circumstance?

All institutions are engaged in more or less formal self-examination, but there cannot be assurance that the interpretation of the past, the evaluation of the present, or the long look into the future is unobscured. All that can be done is to make the best use of the education, experience, and contemplative powers of those who are willing to give some thought to what may lie ahead. In this process the ideas of others, too, should be welcomed, not only because there may be intrinsic value in these, but for another more politic reason. How can one justify accepting the tax money of any citizen while spurning his ideas offered in good faith? There is no harm in considering, even soliciting, advice outside the college walls. How much of it should be accepted is a matter to be determined after deliberation.

In these times universities have the advantage of a great upsurge of interest in all education. Whether this is inspired by fear is beside the main point—they are in a strong position to take leadership and have it looked upon favorably by a majority of citizens. But if there should be a feeling that educators are insensitive to, indifferent to, or condescending about the views of persons or groups which have an interest in the university, then there is danger of negating the advantage now enjoyed.

The municipal university, therefore, is free, yet dependent. An impossible situation? Not at all. It must have public support, yet it gets that support by the recognition it gains through exercise of freedom to determine its own objectives and assume community leadership. Time was when a university president was little more than a mendicant in a frock coat, high hat, and stiff collar. Even then one might have heard the now-familiar phrase, "the pursuit of excellence," but the big problem was not excellence. It was survival. Enlightened patronage enables the municipal institution's administrator to worry less about survival and spend more effort toward achieving excellence. It is a desirable trend.

### Diversity in the Municipal University

It has been said that the Athenians preferred that their young people be educated in their native city. This gave them a good grounding in the philosophy and knowledge which would be necessary to them as they came into positions of leadership there. If one of the basic reasons for municipal support is the development of the future leaders in all areas of community affairs, there still is some merit in the Athenian policy. The modern world, however, is much larger than that of Athens, and a provincial institution can never be a truly strong one any more than a provincial community can. There is no reason why the municipal university need be provincial.

These institutions are no more so than many others which never have been subject to the condescending attitude which crops up in such terms as "street car college." Those who take the trouble to find out know that street cars are long gone in most cities, and so is the restricted horizon implied in the charge.

Municipal universities are cosmopolitan. True, they ordinarily do not have huge dormitory facilities, but many of them have enough to produce a cosmopolitan campus population. Many foreign students are enrolled and students come from many states, attracted in part by the professional programs and by the advantages of the city "laboratory."

There are several advantages in encouraging the out-of-town student. He can be selected on a more restrictive admissions basis than the in-town student, and thus not only brings the different point of view but may provide academic incentive in stiff classroom competition. Of course the higher fees charged to out-of-town students (often about the same as at a private college) are a useful source of income. Studies at the University of Toledo show that it would be uneconomical to offer some programs were it not for the nonresident students enrolled in them.

The antidote for provinciality is primarily in the faculty itself. Here the department heads and deans can range as widely as they wish in recruiting their staff members. The varied faculty background is the strongest element in assuring diversity, broad outlook, wide experience, and catholic interests which any good institution must have.

Along with this diversity goes another—the wide range of individual and social needs of the students. A perennial question raised among educators concerns the ability of a university to provide for these student needs and still maintain "quality" programs. Educators associated with municipal universities do not see this as a dilemma, and contend that the word "quality" should be removed from whatever problems or antitheses are implied in the question. They dislike comparing the quality of one institution or program with that of another. They believe the question, as it is posed, often seems to imply that diversity in higher education, such as is necessary on the part of a municipal university, will lead to intellectual impoverishment. On the contrary, they argue, municipal universities can and should teach almost any necessary program with enough intellectual insight to liberate the student from provincial blinders. This is as true of so-called "practical" courses as it is of those labeled "cultural." They need not be mutually exclusive. Many vocations meet no trivial or transient needs. They long have held an essential place in the lives of civilized people; they have a characteristic ethical tradition; they have nursed fine characters; and they have given scope to new ideas. Without scientific knowledge or trained artistic sensibility, many ancient vocations cannot be carried on with any degree of satisfaction. To educate a man in them is to make it possible for him to throw himself into his work with spirit and derive from it stimulation of mind and character. Indeed, there are minds whose energies can be released only by studies with the directly envisaged goal of a technical or a professional training.

Cardinal Newman, in his *Idea of a University*,[3] has expressed what the end of a university course should be:

> A university training aims at raising the intellectual tone of society, at cultivating the public mind, at purifying the national taste, at supplying true principles to popular enthusiasms and fixed aims to popular aspirations, at giving enlargement and sobriety to the ideas of the age, at facilitating the exercise of political power and refining the intercourse of private life.

The problem, then, is one of giving technical subjects a humane direction and inspiration. So, in all programs in municipal universities the demand is for highest quality possible, whether provision is being made for two-year technical education or for a graduate research center. This quality, municipal university educators emphasize, is necessary to satisfy both social and individual needs and to realize the potential of the individual.

James Conant, discussing the primary concern of American education, has said, "Our purpose is to cultivate in the largest number of our future citizens an appreciation both of the responsibilities and the benefits which come to them because they are American and free."

---

3 John Henry, Cardinal Newman, *Select Discourses from The Idea of a University*, ed. May Yardley (New York: Macmillan, 1931), pp. 100–101.

If Americans are to remain free men, education must create an atmosphere of freedom. The nation was founded and made great by men who were free. The contributions of American political thinkers, statesmen, and jurists have been in the great tradition of free men. Diversity in thought has marked the approaches to the solution of political and social problems, which do not lend themselves to the cool test tubes of the laboratory.

There is need also to clarify the matter of providing for a "wide diversity of individual and social needs." Does this mean providing everything for everybody with no common educational core? If so, the municipal university is opposed to it. Whatever provision is made for diversity, the need first is for a high quality program of general education. This is true because general education meets the common social needs of people who must know something of ends, limitations, and methods of science in the scientific age, who must know something of the social order and the methods of social science if they are to live in a democracy, and who must know something of the arts, philosophy, and language if they are to develop themselves as individuals.

Today, however, there are universities that turn out students by the thousands who can sell their superb ability to build tunnels, prepare balance sheets, make case studies, and adapt plastics to various new uses, but who may be lost when it comes to evaluating and adapting themselves to the kinds of life their work is helping to shape. If students acquire mere skills without insight into human history, without the wisdom one finds in literature and the arts, without awareness of nature's dynamic processes imparted by the scientists, they will lack the perspective to live a full life in the changing world.

A great editor, Erwin Canham, has written that "education must help us to awaken to our true commitment in the world." That commitment, said Mr. Canham, "is to individual man and his birthright under God." In the municipal universities, so close to the people, the question must often be asked, "How is higher education living up to this important responsibility?"

Surely if the municipal universities are dealing in terms of a great people's enduring message to mankind, they are concerned with more than some of the byways along the broad avenue opened by higher education. They are concerned with more than the upgrading of waiters or machinists, or even accountants or journalists, as such. The universities are misdirecting their time and effort to the extent that they labor to teach college girls how to iron their laundry while sitting down, or grant degrees to prospective directors of jazz bands. There is a place for such specialized skills, but democracy hardly will prevail because its people have only a certain slick dexterity. The municipal universities, as well as all colleges and universities, must be concerned mainly with ideas and principles.

In municipal universities diversity in the programs designed to achieve general education is essential, since individuals differ so widely in ability and background. There is not, however, diversity in the goal. All formal education, not merely general education, must carefully select its materials. Inevitably, the whole educational process is selective, even eclectic. There is no time to teach everything about anything. There is an endless series of things to know. These are problems primarily of curriculum, or of fashioning the right course for a given student or group of students. They are difficult problems but not insoluble ones. Their solution lies in obtaining sufficient and excellent personnel and a good testing service. They are not insoluble problems unless one calls the task of getting enough good teachers insuperable. On the specialized level the problems are the same—money to attract good people and the imaginative leadership to select them and help them realize their maximum effectiveness.

### Education for Democracy

If one assumes that problems of money and imaginative leadership are solved (inasmuch as this chapter is not to discuss financing higher education or the difficulty of finding the right deans or presidents), several problems still stand out. They are those of time, talent, and opportunity.

*The problem of time.* If the municipal university needs both general and specialized education to provide for the diversity of individual and social needs, how can it provide them in a limited time? Most municipal universities do achieve breadth of education, for it need not consume more than 20 to 30 per cent of the student's educational budget. He may still exercise his own vocational preference; he may select his own majors and minors; but he receives a more broadly based preparation for that large portion of life outside his occupational interest. The problem of time, however, becomes acute in professional colleges. It may be even more so in the technical institutes, which offer a two-year program for a terminal degree. Demands of "practical" technical training tend to keep genuine education out of the curriculum.

Professional colleges run into difficulties in the assignment of priorities to the many possible goals of education. To make the point in concrete terms, consider medical education. There probably is agreement that theoretically it would be desirable for a doctor to be well-educated in the broadest sense. He should not only be technically proficient, but he should have a broad understanding of the world he lives in from an historical, philosophical, sociological, and esthetic viewpoint. But what priority should be assigned to these various facets? Are they all of equal importance? The problem is not that technical competence is not essential—it is, and should be given top priority. A sick person expects the doctor to be professionally competent to be able to treat his illness, just as one who wants to invest in an oil well expects the geologist he consults to know a gusher from a dry well. At the moment of need it matters little whether the physician or geologist beats his wife, votes the wrong ticket, or knows a fossil from a piece of tile. But universities need to educate physicians and geologists who are not only competent in their profession, but also intelligent and useful citizens who do not beat their wives or vote irrationally and who do get some satisfaction out of intellectual and esthetic pursuits.

The formal education of professional men, then, resolves itself into two parts: (1) the general education of the man and (2) the professional education of the man. The second aspect is the concern of the professional schools. While the first aspect is the concern of the undergraduate program, discussion of general education for the profession, therefore, becomes pointless. General education is in the domain of the education of the man, while professional training is superimposed upon it, does not take its place, and does not substitute for it. General education for the student preparing for a profession is no different from general education for all college students.

The answer in the vocational schools attached to municipal universities must be to make vocational courses less a matter of training and more one of education. Experience has shown that business and industry are willing and able to provide on-the-job training. The university is failing to fulfill its function if it concentrates on this training and fails to perform its true function. Its true function is to teach, for example, the principles of magnetism and not all the infinite applications of the magnet in modern technology.

*The problem of talent.* Sometimes, it must be granted, there is not enough high quality. This is as true in teaching as it is in research. Certainly there is no surplus of teachers of the liberal arts who will take the world as it comes and illuminate it with the humanities, the sciences, and history. All universities need teachers in the specialized professions who can bring to the civilizing forces of the liberal arts the qualities of exactitude, precision, critical skepticism, and emancipating doubt.

In research the obvious way to provide the quality is to concentrate effort in certain fields at certain institutions. If Syracuse University has an outstanding graduate school of citizenship, it would be unwise to compete with it at Rochester or Buffalo; rather, it would be wise to build up other specialized programs at these institutions. To maintain a program of high quality does not require inter-institutional competition. Surely the land grant colleges offer eloquent testimony to this. Some educators at the University of Toledo questioned the wisdom of the trustees of a neighboring university when they recently authorized the establishment of a college of engineering. With Ohio Northern University (a private institution) and the University of Toledo, each only a few miles away and growing in resources and prestige, it would seem reasonable to make those institutions even better, rather than compete with each other. In other words, every university should not have to offer everything. An alternative, where geography permits, is to join forces. In certain areas there are not enough students to make an administrator feel justified in spending the money necessary for a faculty of the highest quality. There is little reason why Columbia

University and New York University, or the University of Chicago and Northwestern University should not have a joint graduate department in a subject such as Germanics or Oriental literature. However good these departments may be now, they would be better combined and hence could meet the needs of society and the individual student better.

Does American education as it is presently constituted, one may ask, serve best the needs of its students and the needs of the world in which those students will play their parts as Americans and as members of a world-wide fraternity of men and women? A thousand variations of the answer lie in the minds and hearts of every thousand educators who face the issue. Each of these answers has validity and, from the philosophical point of view, an emphatic "yes" seems every bit as valid as a "no." Yet, from a practical viewpoint a "yes" is not as good as a "no," and furthermore it is dangerous and actually negative. It implies a smug satisfaction which can prevent development and progress. Only by answering a resounding "no" to this one question can an educator spur himself on to the restless quest for adjustment and improvement which is imperative today. The smugly satisfied have no place in education. Educators must be dissatisfied, constantly and militantly, with basic premises and techniques. They must be dissatisfied with the end results if they are to meet effectively the urgent demands of society. American educators are not doing the job as they should; they are not serving best the needs of their students and of society. What they must seek to do is to continue to grow, continue to change, try the new without undue rejection of the old and established. They must continue to experiment and explore, continue the difficult process of keeping pace with a changing world. They need to continue to handle, as mature men and women, all the frictions, dissensions, and hurts, which such growth and change inevitably engender.

The task of training students for their roles in a changing world is not easy. It demands primarily that education itself must change to keep pace with that world. Educators do not always know how to do that.

J. Martin Klotsche, Provost of the University of Wisconsin-Milwaukee has said:

Urban universities must resist . . . academic isolation, what-ever its cause may be. We cannot afford to look out upon the con-fusions of the world from the soundproofed walls and ivory towers of isolation and neutrality and insist that we are engaged in too grand an enterprise to find time to respond to the urgencies of the world outside.

. . . the urban university . . . can hold up to the view of the community a profile of itself that has the vantage point of perspec-tive and reason. It can examine the metropolis in its totality, seeing one problem in its relationship to the whole of the urban scene. It can identify both the shortcomings and the accomplishments of the community. . . . It can rise above the local prejudices that stand in the way of progress. It can see beyond the political fragmentation that characterizes so many of our metropolitan areas. It can be a constructive critic, a standard setter, a balancing force. It can blaze new trials, it can stand over and above the tumult and shouting of the market place. It can speak out boldly on matters of principle and bring clarity to community thought in a climate free of bias and emotion. It can identify not only what is and can be, but what should be. . . . By its very nature it can bring urbanity and sophistication to the metropolitan area it serves.[4]

Educational methods, attitudes, techniques and philosophies that served in the past may or may not serve in the present and fu-ture. Knowledge clarified by past great thinkers and educators to meet needs of a hundred years ago or even fifty years ago may or may not be adequate today. Today's students are tomorrow's citi-zens—and who can gauge the demands of tomorrow's world? One thing that is known, however, is that an over-deference to tradition will not suffice.

A modern university has this primary function: to continue as an orderly institution, without discarding its framework of administra-tive and scholarly tradition, and without changing that framework so drastically as to risk chaos. But while surviving as an orderly institution, the university must also be experimental. It must be progressive, inventive, and ever ready to try the new and unproved, exactly as must all the world.

*The problem of opportunity.* If X university (private) has a

---

[4] J. Martin Klotsche, at the Annual Meeting, Association of Urban Universities, Cincinnati, Ohio, November 7, 1960.

college of engineering and the tuition is $800 a year and Y university (state) has a college of public administration and the tuition is $150 a year, equality of opportunity does not exist. Certain young men who might contribute to society as engineers never would make their contribution. If society needs engineers, it seems proper for the state to provide a college of engineering with nominal fees or to assume the responsibility for that college of engineering at X university and reduce its fees. An alternative would be to arrange for some form of subsidy with a guarantee that high standards will be maintained.

In education in a democracy everyone must be given an opportunity to seek out the contribution that he alone can make. Intellectual individuality and freedom of thought and opinion must be stressed.

A democracy's best insurance that its citizens will be educated for democracy lies in the public schools—from the elementary grades to the university. Whatever its weaknesses, education remains the hope of the race. Progress will be made only through learning.

Democracy in education means only that all should have the opportunity of shaping themselves in accordance with standards of excellence previously established. It is for the schools to proclaim and uphold these standards. Only by remaining faithful to their mission will they maintain their own self respect or better the prevailing philosophy of work. As matters now stand in American education, one can say that never have so many managed to get by on so little.

For many years municipal universities have attracted thousands of citizens who worked for something better than they could achieve in the day-by-day struggle for livelihood. Municipal universities are aware of their deep and continuing obligation to make higher education available to all young people with the ability to profit by college work. The absence of hide-bound tradition among the faculties of municipal institutions also contributes to the development of the professional tradition which protects higher education. Indeed, without a careful nurturing of this tradition higher education would fail just as science and art would without freedom.

It would be difficult to put in more forceful words the comments of Robert C. Hoover of Wayne State University, speaking on the role of the university in the big city. He said:

> The valid image [of an urban university] rejects . . . the concept that it exists to give a minimum higher educational experience to those who can afford no better . . . We seek to make it a thing as close to perfection as can possibly be produced by putting our best ideals to work in the immediate practical situation. It is to be a first-class institution, engaged in the most dedicated way to the discovery of knowledge and the best development of the knowledge which we already possess.
>
> This means, in turn, that the urban university must be internally and externally cosmopolitan. It must be broadly inclusive of the best obtainable resources of faculty and staff both within the provincial community of which it is a part, within its own urban region, and within the world-wide community of scholarship and research. Thus, if one only accepts the limited objective of serving well the student needs of the immediate local community, it soon becomes obvious that even to pursue this narrow aim properly, it is necessary that the university be a nation-serving institution with broad contacts of scholarly concern in every corner of the civilized world.
>
> Local students cannot be served well by a university which fails to be a full-fledged university in its own right. It is no break to the urban university student to get the reputation of having earned his degree in an institution which is not known beyond the city limits, which was, in fact, established to dispense educational charity . . .[5]

5 Robert C. Hoover, in a conference on "The University and the City-Planning and Urban Renewal," Wayne State Univ., Detroit, Mich., January 30, 1961.

# CHAPTER III

# Community Responsibility of the Municipal University

The existence of a diversified university in an industrial community confers a number of assets upon industry. Are these assets worthy of financial recognition? In other words, can a clear relationship between these assets and the effective conduct of business and industrial enterprise be established? The cultural and intellectual opportunities provided by a university greatly facilitate the anxious task of recruitment. A university is one of the 'fringe benefits' that is offered at no expense to employees and their families. The university itself acts as a recruiting agency. In . . . many . . . cities, it is the most important single source of doctors, teachers, nurses, and highly qualified employees in commerce and industry. In its role of cooperative and fertile center of the complex of hospitals and other health agencies the medical school creates a larger total of healthy working days, increases life expectancy and combats the ravages of tension and overwork in executives.[1]

## Mutual Assistance

The community supplies its municipal university with some of its income, many of its students, its governing board, some of its faculty, its lay advisers, and many of its friends and critics. It furnishes jobs for students and graduates of the institution and patrons for the numerous events of public interest under university sponsorship, ranging from football games to Shakespearean productions.

In return, the university does many things for the community. It provides educational opportunity for young and old; it maintains a flow of technically trained personnel into business and industry; it educates men and women for the professions so there is less likelihood of shortages in these vital areas; it provides men and women for community leadership in every conceivable kind of organization

---

[1] Cornelis W. DeKiewiet, "The Necessary Price of Leadership," *The Educational Record,* July 1958.

and in government. It makes the city more attractive for those who may wish to locate there; it keeps in the city considerable sums of money which might go elsewhere if young people could not go to college at home. It aids business and industry through research and provides in-service training for its personnel. It gives all the citizens an opportunity to enjoy recreational activities in sports, music, drama, and art. And above all it provides a cultural and educational focus.

Administrators of municipal universities are made aware daily of their responsibilities to the community. These responsibilities are many and they are personal as well as institutional. This chapter deals with some of the broad responsibilities of the university as a whole, with special note of responsibilities in a political area, public service, and in research.

The strength of a democratic society lies in its ability to train and replace its leaders in all fields of activity. This principle was recognized many decades ago in the establishment of public schools in every city and village. It has continued to be recognized in this country by the establishment of a university in every large city. Every census shows that America is becoming more and more an urban civilization. In 1790 one out of twenty inhabitants lived in an urban area. In 1960 three out of five lived in urban areas and many more were employed there. Modern cities are the result of applied science and technological innovation. Their survival and prosperity pose challenging problems of human relations and further scientific progress. It is no accident that for large cities universities are as necessary as waterworks, roads, and schools.

The municipal or urban university is a direct result of industrialization and urbanization. It is an institution that provides for the educational needs and desires of its clientele by adapting its resources to the geographic convenience of the people. The programs of municipal universities are designed to meet the needs of their respective communities as manufacturing and commercial centers interested in the arts and culture as well. The prosperity of a business and industrial city depends upon the success of its economic enterprise. Competent manpower is essential for this success. To grow and prosper a city must have engineers, business leaders, and lawyers. To be a better place to live it must have school teachers and citizens who assume the responsibility for community leadership and appreciate the finer things in American culture.

The programs of municipal universities are aimed at meeting these needs. The small and medium sized firms in large cities cannot depend upon "imported" manpower recruited from other parts of the country or even upon the return of natives who have been educated elsewhere. Recognition of the importance of a municipal university engineering program to help meet the manpower problem is shown by the scholarships established by industrial firms to encourage more local residents to enter this field. These are a good investment when a good majority of the graduates will remain in the community where they have their roots. Likewise, there is a great stimulus to an engineering college in an urban setting. Engineering is concerned with the application of science, and it thrives best when there is a clear channel of communication between teachers, students, and practicing engineers. Without the motivation of the proximity of industry, engineering education tends to become somewhat sterile. With such motivation, education is powerful and effective.

Students in a municipal university located in an industrial center have the opportunity not only to earn part of their college expenses by working in industry but also, of greater importance, they may gain valuable experience by learning the factory worker's point of view and by having firsthand contact with industrial operations through inspection trips taken to a variety of industries.

It is not surprising that in 1906 cooperative education was started at the University of Cincinnati. This plan works best in an area offering plenty of close-to-home jobs. President Walter Langsam also points out that with this program the University is able to accommodate about 30 per cent more students with the same faculty and facilities.

The faculty profits immeasurably by professional contact with the practicing engineer; this is achieved through active participation in the affairs of the local sections of the various technical and professional societies. Also, through consultation there is opportunity for intimate contact with certain of the industries or engineering-design firms. Sponsorship of research is more readily obtained by the faculty member of a municipal engineering college because of the interest of the company or group of companies in the work of the college and loyalty to the institution as a whole, and because of easy and complete communication between research team and sponsor. A tremendous advantage of the highly qualified municipal institution is the fund of teachers made available to it on a part-time basis from the outstanding practicing engineers and scientists employed in the area.

The graduate program is also strengthened by the close cooperation with industry that the municipal university enjoys. This works both ways, as do all the advantages: the presence of a strong educational institution permits industry to recruit bright, ambitious young men for its design, research, and development activities; the opportunity for graduate study and the reciprocal stimulation from exchanging similar ideas will attract young men to one company in preference to a company that may offer higher salary but is not located where the intellectual appetites of the student may be nourished.

Municipal universities have a particular responsibility in their relations with the public schools, for a practical development stemming from the organization and establishment of a municipal university is the many contacts which grow between the public schools of the city and the city university. City public schools send the majority of their college-bound students to the municipal university, and in turn the majority of the university's graduates return to various occupations within the city, including teaching.

At present in the city of Toledo, for instance, more than 75 per cent of the teaching force in the public schools are graduates of the University of Toledo, and more than 80 per cent of the administrative staff were prepared by the University's College of Education. Each year the College of Education contributes from one-fifth to one-fourth of its graduating class to the Toledo public schools. No other school system in the Toledo metropolitan area, Ohio, or Michigan receives as large a percentage of candidates prepared for teaching by the University. This situation is not unique, for other municipal universities perform a similar role in their various communities.

It may be argued that this is not an ideal system, that it would be preferable for teachers in a city system to come from the widest possible cross section of institutions of higher education. Indeed, this is preferable, but competition for promising new teachers is just as severe as it is for more experienced ones of proved merit. In such a situation a city which has a good source of supply at hand is fortunate.

Another close relationship between the public schools and the university occurs as the teacher education program of the university utilizes the public school system for professional laboratory experiences for its students. Public school classrooms and administrative offices serve as the teaching laboratories for college students. Public school teachers and administrative personnel provide guidance and instruction for future teachers and administrators.

Some public school–municipal university relationships spring from the organization of the governing boards which may overlap, some through the personal contacts between board chairmen or the superintendent of schools and the president, or the administrative officers of the two organizations, no matter if there are legal ties or not. Mutual interest in the field of teacher training makes it possible for each to make the best possible use of the facilities of the other.

Of greatest importance is the bond which develops between the public schools and the city university through services the university can provide the schools. College faculty members frequently serve as consultants for public school projects. Public school teachers are free to come to the university for advice and aid from their former teachers and to take advantage of various courses offered by the university. Services of the teacher placement bureau are of vital importance to alumni who desire to improve their own situations. The municipal universities provide counseling and testing services, advice in audio-visual teaching, child study laboratories, and other opportunities which can be of very real service to nearby schools. Certainly the proximity of the teacher education institution and the public school system is bound to affect each greatly.

The opportunities for follow-up and continuous service to its graduates would appear to be enhanced in the municipal university setting, and the nearness of such facilities promotes their more intensive use.

Sufficient manpower for all the professions is a responsibility of the municipal institution. Its alumni are needed to fill the gaps created by the loss of older practitioners and by increasing demands as a result of expanding population. The young man or woman educated in his home city is more likely to stay there than one who broke most of the ties with his own community when he went away to college at age eighteen or nineteen.

Figures based upon nearly a thousand returns in a study made of graduates of the College of Business Administration at the University of Toledo show that 72 per cent of the respondents still lived in the city's metropolitan area.[2] Earlier checks on other professions show similar trends, despite the fact that prospective graduates of the municipal university are wooed with fervor by recruiters from business and industry (and education as well) from across the nation.

In the legal profession about two-thirds of those entering the practice of law in Toledo during recent years obtained either their prelegal or their legal education at the University. In the medical profession approximately one-third of the members of the Academy of Medicine received their premedical work at the University, and more than four-fifths of the registered pharmacists in greater Toledo are graduates of the University of Toledo.

In recognizing that most of these circumstances apply also to other institutions which depend upon proximity for a good-size segment of enrollment, one must consider the added factor of the financial concession enjoyed by the student at the municipal university. If the ranks of the professions are well-filled in these cities, some of the credit must go to the tax support which makes it possible for many youths to reach their goals.

The same advantage exists in the other public universities, especially those in the big cities. The state university in an urban setting will have a large commuter population and in other ways serve the same functions as a municipal university for nearby residents. The principal difference is that in this case the subsidy comes from the entire state. Thus, the taxpayers who support a municipal university also aid in the support of state institutions which may be serving about the same purposes in another locality where the citizens are not subject to the additional tax burden.

---

[2] Robert D. Mason, *College of Business Administration Report on Alumni* (Toledo, Ohio: University of Toledo, January 1960).

### The Responsibility for Public Service

One of the greatest of all the functions of municipal universities is their contribution to public service. This is entirely logical, for universities exist for that service. Government and universities can be mutually beneficial. They should maintain close contacts. There is close correlation between the amount of financial support provided by the city government and the type and extent of relations between the university and the city government.

Universities which are dependent on annual appropriations by the city's governing body probably have much closer contact and more direct relations with the city officials than universities, such as Toledo, which obtain financial support from sources over which city officials have little or no control. Municipal universities which are dependent upon an annual appropriation will do much better if they can develop a precedent for receiving a lump sum appropriation from the city, which will become part of the total revenue of the university and can be spent as determined by the university's board of directors.

While city councils normally resist such lump sum appropriations, as some state legislatures also do, the lump sum appropriation is desirable from the standpoint of the university receiving the funds. If a legislative body attempts to get into details of a university budget, it may make changes in items about which it has little or no knowledge, in order to effect what it believes are economies. The governing body of the city should have confidence in the board of directors of the university and should allow it a rather free hand in how it spends the money which it has available.

While even a privately supported institution of higher learning in a metropolitan area has an obligation to serve the community in which it is located, a university receiving substantial public support probably has an even greater obligation, especially to the particular governmental agency which is supporting the school. More specifically, the city may look to the university for special advice and assistance in technical fields in which the university has qualified persons on its staff—engineers, for example. At the same time the city probably should not expect to receive a great amount of consulting service unless provision is made for this in the budget.

In connection with the university's obligation to serve the community, the university should encourage its faculty and other staff members to participate in community affairs of all types. Not only will this help dispel the ivory tower theory many have about faculty members, but it will make available to the community and its many organizations and agencies the extensive background and experience of university people.

When the university is spending tax money, it would appear that there must be opportunity for the development of combined efforts such as the joint purchasing arrangement in Cincinnati, participated in by the University of Cincinnati, the City of Cincinnati, and the Cincinnati City School district.

The university, as a public institution, should observe and be governed by all the laws of the community which would affect it as a private institution or which affect private agencies. Zoning laws, for instance, should be observed by public institutions, as should regulations relating to planning in the community. The university should not seek special treatment merely because it is a public institution.

Similarly, the university should coordinate its physical planning with planning of other governmental agencies. The university should not, for instance, plan a large parking lot with access to streets designated by the community's planning agency as residential streets. This is not to say that the university should not seek amendments in the master plan of the community or the zoning ordinance. The university, however, should be treated the same as any other interests would be in like circumstances.

Not the least of the responsibilities of municipal universities is their obligation to convince young men and women that public service is the foundation of citizenship and the only real assurance for the continuation of our free society. An effective government requires the best talents available. How is it to get them? It must have people who reject the idea of public service as a sinecure, but instead dedicate themselves to even greater constructive and useful service to the people. The importance of this principle on the part of municipal universities cannot be overemphasized. The increasing complexity of modern social problems requires the constant flow into service of young men and women who are well-informed and well-educated. It is important, too, that this preparation by the municipal university be scholarly and objective. The American Assembly has stated: "Competent people are needed in state government. More of our able men and women must be attracted to the top administrative and professional positions, for they are among the most influential persons in setting the whole tone of state administration."

The word "city" could be substituted for "state" in the above quotation and it would have special meaning for municipal universities. Education of competent men and women for public service is one of the principal tasks to which municipal universities address themselves. Their efforts stem from the fact that top-level city officials see the need for trained public officials. The universities also recognize that a trained corps of potential administrators is vital to public service and that many communities have not been attracting their share of young people oriented toward government as a major interest.

Coupled with this is the growing demand of the potential and actual city employees themselves for additional training in their specialties. This demand is in keeping with what one authority on administration has called the most significant indication of the real possibility of continuing improvement of public service. Municipal universities recognize this responsibility and some invest sizable amounts of funds in their programs to upgrade city employees. Just what have been the objectives?

Many city administrations believe that there is a major benefit both to the individual employee and to his department of service, as well as to the city service generally, in seeking out every year some of the younger, permanent employees who already have shown an unusual interest in, and aptitude for, administration. The enlightened municipalities have proclaimed their faith that those individuals can increase administrative skill and vision through participating in adult education programs offered by their universities.

The cities also recruit recent graduates who have had specialized training but who want the broad training in government service. Training is provided to bridge the gap between theory and practice. A major objective is to retain as many as possible in the service of the city. The practice is a contribution to good government generally, and even if the benefited employee leaves government service, there is still a major contribution in the form of a better-informed citizen.

A question logically arises as to why a city should invest its money, energies, and the efforts of some of its best people in such programs. The policy is related to a realization by leaders of the city government of the truth in the comment by John Stuart Mill that, "With small men, no great thing can really be accomplished." The training programs in which municipal universities participate are dedicated to the employee's growth, so that he may add to the city service his unique skills and abilities.

American leaders are coming rapidly to a realization that the demands of all government, if it is to be good, require that public service must command the best talents that can be had and make them an integral part of the administrative system. The critical need for better career service in administration has been dramatically shown. There are not enough trained government executives to meet even the most urgent requirements.

To such a problem there is an answer, even though it involves long-range effort over many years rather than a simple crash program that would solve everything overnight. As York Willbern has put it, "The most significant key to effective management of the public business is people—what kind of people and how they work."

"If administrative tasks," he said, "can be done by people of high competence, strongly motivated, possessed of the expertness and consistency of approach produced by continuous tenure, responsive to the public interests and desires, and effectively led, there will be fewer obstacles that cannot be overcome."

It would be hard to justify local support of a university unless it were apparent that there are mutual benefits derived from the association. These benefits are quite clear. Each party to the compact gains something it would not otherwise enjoy, and both are the stronger and more vigorous for it.

There is a need in American cities for well-educated leadership. What more appropriate place is there to look for this leadership than to the municipal university itself? Those who ponder the future of the great metropolitan complexes recognize the role higher education is destined to play:

> The college of the future will be much more closely knit to the community. Indeed, most of the new institutions which inevitably must come into being will grow directly out of the community. Their students will usually live at home. They will not have to set up an artificial college community in which to practice; they will be able to function as participants in a real community from the very beginning of their college careers without bothering about synthetic problems. And their transition from college students to adult citizenship will be virtually imperceptible . . .

> The closer ties to the community will have real effect upon the traditional feelings about a college education. Much of the glamour and social prestige value will disappear, since many aspects of present campus life will be discarded as non-essential. A good deal of the social life of the student will center around the community and the college together, rather than on the college alone . . .[3]

## The Research Dilemma

The activities of any university—by definition—must include a comprehensive, vigorous, and productive research program. The effects of such a program on the instructional mission of the institution are beneficial and desirable. The extension of man's knowledge of himself, the university, and his place in it is a function of the municipal university which actually is of equal importance to the giving of instruction.

In the conduct of research, as with the curriculum, there is need constantly to examine the program to insure that the variety, amount, and type of research activity conducted by the faculty members are consistent with the aims of the university and will further its development. There must also be assurance that portions of academic research activities do not heedlessly divert energies from the traditional and rightful concerns of a municipal university. In the area of research these concerns have been with the conduct of basic research as opposed to developmental activities—with the development of the *principle* and not the development of the *device*.

Unfortunately, economic and scientific developments of recent

---

[3] Samuel B. Gould, "New Frontiers for Higher Education." An address at an Antioch College assembly, January 27, 1955. From Association of Urban Universities, *Newsletter* (May to June, 1955).

years have boosted greatly the cost of sustaining these enriching and stimulating experiences on the campuses. The result has been that educational institutions, both public and private, have been forced to develop new sources of funds for the support of their research programs.

For the most part, these supplementing funds have come from three major groups. The rising number of foundations represents an increasingly important source of support for academic research. These organizations, recognizing their public responsibilities, have given generously of their "venture capital" to finance the scholar's ceaseless search for knowledge. Evidence of the wisdom of this policy can be found in the achievements in every area of academic research.

The pressing urgencies of national defense during and since World War II catapulted the Federal government into fiscal leadership in the support of both basic and applied research activities. Seeking the university's traditions and experience, the government channeled to educational institutions a sizable portion of these scientific subsidies to underwrite the research expenses of many scientist-teachers. Without this enormous expenditure of Federal money it would hardly have been possible to develop and finance the vast programs such as those in nuclear research. It is possible that the by-products of these investigations undertaken in the cause of national defense may yet be of significantly greater importance than the weapons which stimulated the research.

The third major new source of assistance to the universities, and particularly municipal universities, is the larger corporations of American industry and their industrial associations. A general recognition of the contribution of new scientific discoveries in generating the profits produced from a constantly rising consumer standard of living has multiplied the contacts between campus and industrial laboratories. Even more recently, an encouraging awareness of the social obligations of business is stimulating greater support of fundamental research and other academic activities for which no immediate financial returns are expected.

Each of these relatively new and immensely valuable sources of financial assistance for academic research programs has, to some extent, shifted both the nature of research on the campus and the conditions under which it is carried out. This redirection comes about partly because each new donor, by means of more-or-less restrictive grants, actually assumes partial control of the institution's research. Such a division of authority, while understandable and perhaps necessary, imposes severe administrative burdens on the officers of the research-conducting institutions.

This shifting in the base of the research fiscal support to industry and to government is tending to encourage the redirection of the research to the short-term, limited-objective, predictable-outcome program. True, the short-term program undoubtedly reflects the research needs and objectives of both business and of the national welfare. But it must be remembered that too much attention to this type of research can result in serious distortion of research aims and neglect of vital activities in the forwarding of basic research. Indeed, this overemphasis on what has been called "projectivitis" reflects the grave misunderstanding of the nature of the research process and the relationship of the university to the furtherance of knowledge. It has been truly stated that if the researcher knows where he is going, he is not conducting research.

The spectacular developments of the past generation in the physical and life sciences are dependent on discoveries of the intellectual adventurer moving beyond the boundaries of human understanding. His major concern is the satisfaction of his own curiosity. To cite the most obvious example, thermonuclear fission is a direct result of attempts to explain certain inadequacies of Newton's laws in describing the physical universe. Yet, it is possible to be blinded to the importance of this vital portion of the research spectrum by the dazzling brilliance of the overhead percentage figure of a sponsored research contract. Thus, an institutional administration may fail to evaluate proposed research against the interests of the faculty and graduate students.

Paradoxically, in an age of science which owes its greatest accomplishments to the swift reaches of the gifted mind, the fundamental researcher, free to study what he wants and to write about what he finds, is increasingly rare. This is true at a time when research activity on American campuses is at its peak. Today, the intellectual pioneer whose results are impossible to predict in specific terms, and difficult to evaluate except in retrospect, may easily be unknowingly sacrificed. He is sacrificed to make room for the new industry-supported institute, or Federal prototype-development laboratory. Yet, it is well to remember that the traditional habitat of the searcher for first principles is the university campus and laboratory.

Experience demonstrates, time and again, that the scientist who addresses himself to the basic problems of life and matter has served mankind usefully and well. There is little danger that an emphasis on basic research will drive necessary and desirable portions of the applied research programs from university campuses. Certainly, a productive balance of research activities is desirable. It should be maintained, if only to assure a continuing supply of trained scientists and the fruitful contact between all researchers, in universities, industry, and government.

The danger lies, rather, in the other direction: that the large, planned, contract research programs will determine the research atmosphere of university campuses. Institutional administrators must avoid applying to both basic and applied research men the same standards of evaluation, the same qualifications of ability, the same budgetary methods and procedures. Above all, care must be taken to make certain that all factors of importance in directing the course of modern research—such as the needs of industry, the demand for national defense, the growing tendency of the university administration under pressure of limited budgets to insist on clearly defined objectives—do not overwhelm and obliterate the rarest element in the research process: the discovery of general principles governing natural and social phenomena.

Certainly, it is the special province of the university to provide conditions that are favorable for basic and fundamental research. The university must see that such work is encouraged, by protecting and nurturing the traditional freedoms of control, of subject, of publishing, and of discussion. University administrators can best manifest such encouragement by a constant review of research programs to insure that some significant part of the research activities undertaken by the faculty will be out of curiosity rather than compulsion. The conduct, protection, and encouragement of basic research are a major concern of the municipal universities in these times.

Another administrative pitfall on the path of maintaining a balanced research program lies in the over-reliance for support on one source of funds. For this reason, a university cannot risk leaning too heavily on Federal research funds for the support of its basic research activities. The limited Federal funds supporting such work are always primary targets for congressional economies. Municipal universities must find means of sustaining a vigorous program of basic research supported by other than Federal research funds. This means that efforts must be continued to increase endowment, contributions from industry, and research appropriations.

Constant attention to all these factors affecting a university's research can contribute much to insuring that academic laboratories do not become exclusively research arms of industry and government. As former President Dodds of Princeton University has so tersely and ominously warned, "The universities must not fail in this broad function for no other agency in society will assume it if they do."

Writing in his book *Red Brick University*, the critic Bruce Truscot declared, "The primary aim of the university must be search for knowledge—re-search, as we call it today: not merely actual discovery, not merely even the attempt to discover, but the creation and cultivation of the spirit of discovery." Yes, it may be argued that one of the missions of a municipal university, as of any university, and particularly their graduate schools, is the conduct of research, with the objective of assuring the society quicker and surer mastery over the physical and biological aspects of life.

The university with important community ties, however, dares not lose sight of its dual obligation in research. Its first responsibility is that which falls upon every institution of higher learning in seeking new knowledge. Its second is in connection with its responsibility for service. It is natural that business and industry should look to the university for assistance in solving their problems. It has the facilities and the manpower to do this and it is aware that its own progress is dependent in great measure upon the prosperity of the city which supports it.

Perhaps the most serious single problem facing an urban center today is the maintenance of its economic base. Small and medium sized industries, for instance, face changes in the markets of their products which require considerable redesigning and the development of new products, if these firms are to remain prosperous. The prosperity of the city, in turn, is dependent upon the prosperity of its manufacturing firms. If manufacturing payrolls drop, then employment in commercial and service activities soon responds; if manufacturing payrolls rise, the pick-up is multiplied by pick-ups in these other activities.

Without any lessening of their major responsibility for basic research, the programs of municipal universities also can be geared to be of assistance to local industry on problems of applied research and product development. The professional faculties and laboratory facilities of municipal universities are available to assist their respective communities in research and development. The faculties are familiar with conditions and problems in local industry. They also are familiar with the latest advancements in scientific and theoretical knowledge. For community prosperity it is essential to take advantage of scientific progress, to apply it to community problems, to the design and development of useful products for the manufacturing industries.

The municipal university cannot and should not hope to do all of the city's research, but it is in a position to offer suggestions for applied research to local industries, to perform certain unique and difficult research tasks for which it has special equipment, and to do much of the research which may be needed from time to time by small firms. It is the job of the university to suggest, demonstrate, and stimulate research throughout the community. The more successful research there is in the city, the greater will be its prosperity.

Replies to the questions addressed to municipal university officials indicate an awareness of the responsibility to carry on research of importance to business and industry in that city. But, as one of the respondents writes, "Most research problems, particularly in basic research, do not lend themselves to geographic confinement, and we have made no effort to so confine them." In fact, the practice shows an increasing amount of work in fields which have little or no immediate local importance. To encourage this, some municipal institutions now are providing university funds to support internal research in fields where a sponsor cannot be found or it might be impractical to have one. This is a good indication that these institutions are not losing sight of their first obligation in research.

# CHAPTER IV

## Staffing the Municipal University

. . . the students have a life and a world of their own, an important world to them, and when they meet us in the classroom, they are meeting a person who is not, usually, a representative of what they will become in the future. We are professionals; they are amateurs in learning. . . .

Now I do not wish to underrate the present day college student. He is frequently a lively person with an enquiring mind, fresh in his ideas, bold in his thinking, and more interesting often than the professionally committed graduate student. He is likely to be an important person in the future of our country. He is not our kind, perhaps, but we owe him our care and attention. We owe him an education that our country may be better cared for.[1]

### The Search for Faculty Members

Mentioned earlier in this volume is the fact that careful selection of faculty members can help provide the cosmopolitan atmosphere so necessary to an institution of higher learning. What kind of success do the municipal universities have in attracting and holding capable faculty people? The advantages and disadvantages which influence the decision of a candidate for a position are primarily those related to the urban location rather than to the university itself.

The faculty member with an eye to the future may find the municipal university quite attractive. He is aware of the upward trend of enrollments and the increasing demands to be made upon the urban institutions; he sees opportunity for personal and professional growth and advancement in the city; he recognizes the community as a great reservoir for the enrichment of his courses and of his own life.

Cultural opportunities are great in the city whether one wishes to take an active, creative part in the many phases of the arts or

---

[1] William C. DeVane, in *A Regional Faculty-Orientation Program*, ed. Frederic W. Ness (Washington, D.C.: Association of American Colleges, 1961), p. 62.

whether he merely expects to enjoy them. For some, city life avoids the "glass house" feeling one may get in a smaller community. Perhaps the faculty member and his family can enjoy a more normal life in the comparative anonymity found in the city. One can find a wider range, too, in opportunities for shopping, leisure time activities and entertainment, and in the choice of friends outside the campus circle.

But some are not attracted by these. They dislike city life in general—or perhaps, specifically, they do not relish the traffic, the bigness, the wide cross section of citizens and of students as well. They feel the lack of some of the traditional academic atmosphere, the loss of close relationships with students and colleagues. Some of them fear they may be subject to political or other pressures. Some do not like the possibility of teaching classes in the evening or perhaps even on a Saturday morning.

Whether or not one is attracted to the municipal university is primarily a matter of personal taste. What has this meant in practice to the dean or department head seeking new faculty members? Figures show that the municipal universities are holding up well in this talent hunt. In both the academic years 1959–60 and 1960–61 the municipal universities were surpassed only by the non-public universities in percentage of newly employed full-time faculty members who held the doctoral degree. The figures for the municipal universities are 30.5 per cent and 29.9 per cent for the two years. Actually, the percentage is almost identical for state, land grant, and municipal universities, well above the percentages for all institutions during these years—25.9 per cent and 25.8 per cent.[2]

| Full time newly employed with doctor's degree | | | Total doctorates full time staff |
|---|---|---|---|
| | 1959–60 | 1960–61 | 1953–54 |
| State Universities | 29.3% | 29.7% | 47.6% |
| Non-public Universities | 36.2 | 35.9 | 51.9 |
| Municipal Universities | 30.5 | 29.9 | 44.3 |
| Land Grant Colleges | 30.1 | 29.8 | 42.5 |
| State Colleges | 20.9 | 22.6 | 32.5 |
| Teachers Colleges | 15.9 | 15.9 | 29.9 |
| For all institutions | 25.9 | 25.8 | 40.5 |

[2] Higher Education Series Research Report 1961-R12, *Teacher Supply and Demand in Universities, Colleges, and Junior Colleges 1959–60 and 1960–61* (Washington, D.C.: Research Division, National Education Association, May 1961), p. 15. See the table above.

While these figures are subject to interpretation and explanation, they at least indicate that the Ph.D.'s do not shy away from the municipal university. One would suspect that the element of "municipality" has little to do either with acceptance or rejection of an offer. If the opportunities, personal and professional, are there and the salary is right, the type of control in most cases becomes a minor factor.

Salary schedules in municipal universities compare favorably with those in other types of institutions (see the AAUP Bulletin, Vol. 47, No. 2, Summer 1961). Actual salaries vary because they depend somewhat upon the size of the community. The metropolis offers stern competition for able people in scientific, business, and some professional fields. Consequently, there cannot be too great a gap, lest the university find its staff lured away to more lush pastures right at home.

It might be cynical to suggest, as some have done, that "dedicated" is merely a euphemism for "underpaid." Almost any faculty member, no matter how much or little he is paid, will at least be tempted by offers of more money, and some of them do yield. But the urban situation does provide ways in which the professional salary may be enhanced. Commercial consulting and research can be profitable sidelines for some faculty members. Both are done more easily in an urban setting than on a campus far removed from a large city. As a result, policy toward such activity often is not too strict, it becomes a fringe benefit and sometimes a most attractive one. The right to take advantage of these kinds of opportunities may even be included as part of a professor's contract.

At the 1960 meeting of the Association of Urban Universities, President David M. Delo of the University of Tampa reported for a discussion group on what sometimes has been called multiple employment of faculty members. He said it seemed the consensus that outside employment of faculty should, in general, be confined to one day per week and that this employment should contribute in some fashion to the continuing and enhanced competence of the instructor. He noted that in many areas this outside work is highly desirable because it may keep the faculty member in touch with new developments in his field.[3]

---

[3] The Association of Urban Universities, "Summary of Proceedings of the Forty-sixth Annual Meeting," ed. Doris O'Brien (Cincinnati, Ohio, 1960).

## It Takes All Kinds

All kinds of faculty members are to be found on the campus of the municipal university. They run the gamut of quality, skill, interest, dedication, age, experience, or any other characteristic one might name. There are master teachers and inept laboratory assistants. There are great scholars and scientists and mere time-servers. There are oldsters awaiting retirement and youngsters looking for a new position one rung higher on the academic ladder.

Here as elsewhere one finds divided loyalties. The faculty member may feel that his future depends upon the discipline rather than upon the institution, so he stakes his career upon the progress he can make in his subject matter field rather than his service as a member of the university. When this happens, he can gain recognition as a scholar, but he may lose some of his value as a member of faculty committees concerned with problems of the institution as a whole.

Perhaps it is not really a digression at this point to note that the rather common complaint about "too many administrators" is related to this situation. There was a time when faculties were almost completely responsible for the operation of most institutions of higher learning. But the scholar found that some of the responsibilities of keeping the establishment running smoothly not only were time-consuming but also not very inspiring. Somebody had to do the job in order that the professor might be more free to teach, study, write, and search for the truth. He found little appeal in academic housekeeping. But faculty members cannot disregard all their responsibilities to the institution as a whole. Individualists though they may be, they still must help maintain some semblance of cooperation and order within the programs of an institution. There are responsibilities concerning the university which they cannot ignore or delegate. They cannot fall back upon what President Paul C. Reinert of St. Louis University calls the "professional soldier" theory wherein you hire somebody to do a job and everybody else then sits back and waits for results.[4]

The greater opportunity for outside interests and the reluctance

---

[4] *The Advancement of Understanding and Support of Higher Education* (Washington, D.C.: American College Public Relations Association, 1958), p. 62.

of some to carry much responsibility for the general conduct of the institution increases the burden on those who still are available and willing to assist with these latter chores. This same situation makes it necessary to employ more people to perform some of the tasks which once were divided among faculty members.

Faculty members in the liberal arts may have somewhat fewer outside opportunities for consulting and research than their colleagues in business administration, engineering, or some other fields. This kind of situation can set up internal stress and strain. The arts college man who takes on a time-consuming committee assignment, probably without extra pay, resents the fact that another faculty member cannot serve because he is busy consulting—for pay. And possibly the professor of engineering or business administration, because of the law of supply and demand, is receiving a higher salary in the first place. This does not make for happy faculties or administrators.

It is possible, too, that one deeply engrossed in his own field may take a somewhat intolerant view of students, who, as Dean DeVane pointed out, are, in general, not "our" kind, having no interest in becoming scholars and/or professors. The faculty member who is unaware of this difference or who admits it only grudgingly, may not be happy with the undergraduate student body found on the campus of a municipal university. He would be far better off in a graduate school or at a college where students are selected from a narrower stratum of high school graduates. There he would at least have more homogeneity among those in his classes.

Is the scholarly faculty member, interested in good teaching, likely to find the municipal, or urban, institution a frustrating place because of the nature of its student body? Will he find that this diversity begets a relaxation of academic standards? The question as to the extent of lowered standards brings some interesting responses from those close to the scene:

> There are mingled feelings about relaxation of academic standards because of a broad range of abilities in the student body.
> If so, it does not appear in the grading reports. . . . It would be normal to expect that institutions with very selective standards of admission can achieve higher standards generally.
> The feeling among some of the faculty that they must relax their

academic standards because of the nature of the student body may not be deliberate or conscious, but it is so. It is not, however, prevalent enough to become a problem.

The faculty apparently is quite demanding, judging from failures and dropouts. Nevertheless, faculty members are aware that a fairly large portion of the student body is employed part time.[5]

This author's own observation is that quality is where you find it, that it varies from department to department and from college to college, and it can be found in the municipal university just as readily as in most others. The municipal colleges in New York City have nurtured "in their undergraduate years more future scientists who received Ph.D.'s from 1936 to 1956 than any other college or university in the United States, and more future scholars in the arts, humanities and social sciences, [than any] except the University of California."[6]

Teaching in a municipal institution in a great city can be challenging and exciting. Even though the faculty member is not preparing most of his students for scholarly pursuits, he is guiding them as citizens at a time in history when a serious, thoughtful citizenry is needed as never before.

For the person who finds stimulation in metropolitan life, the rewards of faculty membership in a municipal university are high. There is almost no limit to the status he can make for himself, for in the city there always is need for leadership in the many phases of community activity. This is true of the opportunities within the university, too, for its role in the city cannot but become more important in the years ahead.

## Using the City's Resources

Viewed from the institutional rather than the personal viewpoint, the municipal university is in a unique position in staffing its program. Estimates of the coming shortage of qualified teachers for the nation's colleges and universities range upward of 200,000. The problem of recruiting and keeping faculties is no less urgent than

---

[5] Replies to 1961 questionnaire compiled by author.

[6] Board of Higher Education, *The Proposal for The City University of New York,* January 20, 1961.

that of raising funds for facilities that could physically accommodate potentially doubled enrollments. A classroom without the instructor serves little purpose.

Those who foresee the danger also are quick to cite the real obstacles which make it difficult, if not impossible, to find enough men and women to staff the classrooms. Even with the promise of devices such as TV and the prospective compromise of larger classes, different division of the academic year, more class hours in the days and weeks, there remains an excellent possibility that adequately prepared teachers in sufficient numbers simply will not be available. The loss by the teaching profession of many of its best people to industry and other non-teaching occupations only serves to emphasize the seriousness of the problem. Largely because of better salaries, there is a steady flow of teachers out of the classroom.

Personal observations indicate that there should be a good opportunity to reverse that flow and bolster the ranks of the teaching profession. This involves, among other things, a potentially outstanding contribution by American business and industry to the field of higher education. It could be a more significant contribution than all the corporate contributions to university treasuries combined. The burden would not, however, be on the corporations; rather, the corporations would, at some point, be called upon to encourage, at least in principle, the idea of making vast investments in talent accessible to the institutions.

Reversing the flow of talent from the campus to the corporation does not involve preventing those able and ambitious men who feel the need to make that change from doing so. Rather, there is a channel so that the men already established in business, presumably successful there (or in one of the professions), can obtain information about teaching and the opportunities which may await him at some campus. Municipal universities are alert to the possibilities and call upon the great reservoir of talent in their communities.

This is not to suggest that every businessman potentially is a college teacher; this clearly is ruled out by reasons of individuals' education, abilities, inclinations, incomes, and other factors. Municipal universities by no means believe in a mass raid on business;

that would be undesirable as well as fantastically impossible for many reasons. But it is undeniable that among the millions of college-educated business and professional (non-teaching) men in the country, there are a substantial number who, under the right set of circumstances, do teach and do become actively interested in doing so.

First, all are familiar with higher education from a personal experience which, in most cases, was a successful one. Some of them even may have been teachers earlier in their careers, but this is a side issue not highly relevant in the present discussion.

Second, many of them have demonstrated their concern with the problems of higher education and are receptive to an opportunity to help do something about one of the nation's major problems.

Third, numbers of them have achieved enough material success so they can contemplate without regret a reduction in earnings which university teaching almost surely would entail; often accompanying this, however, is a readiness to taper off in personal activity, into a life and an atmosphere which basically is less demanding in terms of tensions. The almost idealized campus life, the "image" (possibly unfounded) of the relatively leisured life of the professor—these are strong pulls psychologically.

Fourth, many of them have exceptional knowledge, insights and experiences which could truly enrich the academic offerings of many a department. They, of all people, teach out of the wealth of personal experience properly mixed with the theoretical. This reference is not intended to embrace the anecdotal kind of visiting lecturer who occasionally spices, without enriching, a course. A willingness to plan and organize a course offering, and each class meeting in turn, is assumed. The question of insuring that this is the case in individual instances is one of detail for the academic administration to settle satisfactorily.

Fifth, the status of the teacher is open to question, though recent events have done much to tend to reestablish him. Such gains, if they are actual, need to be consolidated and extended. The profession of teaching should be set forth as one of the most honored; this happens to be a necessity for the effort to lure the businessman into teaching and is a natural byproduct of his presence there. These elements must be kept in mind in charting any proposal to bring the businessman to the classroom.

At present one of the most important contributions of the municipal university is the establishment of channels through which the man who may be wondering about the actual market of his talents in education may obtain that information. Officials of municipal universities are in almost daily contact with the business and professional people of their cities. They are constantly on the alert for prospective teachers with ability, and they make this known. The interested businessman, now armed with certain basic information, explores definite and particular possibilities—hardly as a neophyte applicant, but with all the reserve and dignity which his present position demands.

On the reverse side, the college administrator and department head in a municipal university often (and with increasing alacrity) are receptive to a new teacher ready to make the move from the nonacademic world. Much more needs to be done, however.

Included among the possibilities for entrance to the academic field are career officers in the armed forces. It is becoming common that, upon retirement, some of these men look to college teaching as a new opportunity. Sometimes graduate work will be needed, but they have good backgrounds and are financially able to enrich their formal education before entering teaching. Many already are well-qualified in fields such as management, transportation, personnel, various branches of engineering, and sometimes even in areas less closely related to their former activities.

A recent alumni seminar at the University of Toledo brought to the campus graduates who had achieved successful careers in a number of professions. One of their suggestions, from the viewpoint of twenty years after college, was that the value of a faculty member's contribution to his students is enhanced greatly by practical experience in his field or profession. The older man with this experience, who believes that he has an interest in teaching, can soon find out if he has the talent for it also. If he does, the result is mutually beneficial to him, to the students, and to the institution.

A service of real significance to both the college and the individual would be the provision of means whereby experienced men could obtain the necessary information needed to guide them to their professional interests. The need is also to provide part-time or temporary teaching positions (or occasional lectureships) in which the businessman can reassure himself and his prospective employers of his adaptability for the new career.

CHAPTER V

# The Student Body of a
# Municipal University

The urban university has always attracted large numbers of students because of its accessibility to all the great cultural, industrial, financial and research centers located in the urban community, because of its outstanding faculty members drawn from the community, and because it offers the student body greater outside learning opportunities.

With an ever increasing proportion of students coming from lower- and middle-income families and the costs of college education increasing, many students will have to live at home and commute for full- or part-time study. The population of the United States is becoming increasingly concentrated in the metropolitan complexes. The downtown institution, because of its accessibility to transportation facilities, thereby becomes the logical choice for those young people who for economic reasons must remain at home. Similarly, the location of the urban institution makes it the logical choice for evening students because of its proximity to large areas of employment.[1]

## Environment Leaves Its Mark

A college student is a college student, whether of the 1922 or 1962 vintage and whether he attends a municipal university, a private one in a rural setting, or some other kind. But there are differences among institutions which mark the young man or woman who studies there. Some colleges are a little world in themselves. Others are part of a larger community with little of the "self-contained" aspect. The nature of the student body in a municipal university will be affected by a number of factors common to all these institutions but varying in degree from one city to another.

---

[1] Ruth Weinstock, *Space and Dollars: An Urban University Expands* (New York: Educational Facilities Laboratories, 1961), pp. 7–8.

Among these factors are: (1) somewhat less selective admissions than in private schools—thus, a wide range of differences in abilities and in ages among the students; (2) a large commuting population—consequently, a relatively small proportion of students living on the campus; (3) a high percentage of students holding outside jobs, full- and part-time—therefore, large night and part-time enrollments; and (4) a diversity of courses and programs from which the student may choose.

On the average, only about 10 per cent of the students in a municipal university will be campus dwellers. This means that few of them are in the vicinity when classes are not in session. Classes might be held from 8 A.M. until 10 P.M., and sometimes the day is even longer. This spreading out of hours means that there never is a time when all the students, or even a high percentage of them, will be on the campus simultaneously. While this may ease traffic pains, it frustrates attempts to schedule any kind of event in the nature of a mass meeting. Consequently, students complain of lack of interest in student elections and other affairs in which participation by large numbers can be interpreted as a manifestation of school spirit.

Officials in municipal universities report that there is a general feeling among students that school spirit is lacking. This is attributed to the outside interests of students, to the fact that from 50 to 80 per cent of them will be employed part time, and to the feeling that excessive enthusiasm is not a mature trait.

How much loyalty continues among university students for the high schools from which they graduated seems debatable, but there is no doubt but that the off-campus friends, individually and in formal and informal groups, vie with the college for the time and interest of the student in a municipal university.

There is a consensus that student organizations, rather than individuals, are the moving force in promoting campus activity and school spirit. One even finds the suggestion that where so few live on the campus the close fellowship found in fraternities and sororities may take on some added importance in the process of developing the well-rounded personality. It is common experience that the best way to promote interest in a campus activity is to turn these groups loose in competition for a trophy.

There seem to be quite a number of students who feel that the kind of school spirit which is measured in decibels is beneath their dignity. This aversion became especially noticeable when the veterans returned after World War II. It continues partly because of the diverse nature of the urban student body. There is evidence that a student center or union has been a valuable asset in encouraging students to take part in more of the campus life than merely attending classes 15 or 16 hours each week.

Work schedules complicate life for many of the students in municipal universities. The author knew one student who worked a full night shift as a newspaper copy boy while completing his senior-year courses. He finished his courses; but sleeping, he said, was a problem since it was frowned upon both on the job and in his classes. Another senior's day began at 4:30 A.M.; he worked for a radio station, processing the news for early morning broadcasts. For this young man the job not only was good practical experience but also was a necessity, for he was married and the father of a small child.

It is not surprising that the University of Cincinnati, with its cooperative plan, should report 75 per cent of its students employed, but even in universities without this plan the percentage runs nearly this high. Students in evening classes help keep the figure up, and the institution with a majority of men will have a higher percentage working. Women students who have jobs often work for only a few hours one or two evenings or on week ends, many of them as secretaries or clerks.

Academic counselors often must try to adjust class schedules with working hours so the student can do justice to both. A heavy work load means that either the working hours or the course hours will have to be fewer.

Getting to and from jobs and coming to the campus at varying hours make a car a necessity for many students at the urban university. The automobile affects his way of life considerably, for he may have a serious problem of meeting payments, thus aggravating the friction between job and school work.

Students' cars create traffic problems for the campus and for residents of the neighborhood. Parking lots spread and sprawl and multi-level parking garages appear. These and traffic control cost money, so fees have to be charged for the service. For reasons of safety and best utilization of space, enforcement has to be increased. More fines are assessed and collected and more protests arise to mar friendly relations between administration and students. If there is limited space available, student-faculty relations are strained, too, in the scramble for preferred parking places. At the resident school the situation can be alleviated by forbidding the use of motor vehicles or restricting their use to certain students, upperclassmen for example.

Some of the foregoing observations are underscored by Dean Haack of Washington University:[2]

> To most observers our campuses are not particularly different from others in the things that show up in the catalogues: our organization, our faculty and curriculum, or even the visible structure of our student personnel services. The differences show up most clearly in the patterns of campus life and student activity. As has already been pointed out, we *look* and *feel* different. We differ most noticeably from the standpoint of conventional campus activity standards because of:
> 1. Less overt mass participation, less tangible manifestation of school spirit—low level "rah-rah" dimension.
> 2. The preponderance of "street car" students, i.e., those whose student life cycle omits campus participation beyond the classroom.
> 3. The fact that the undergraduate student body is less central in the institution—its typical focus diluted by large numbers of part-time, graduate and professional school students.
> 4. Competition with interests and attractions of the community— "Big League" activities.
> 5. The shortened activity day.
> 6. The problem of living in two communities.
> The realistic setting of the urban campus with a program adequately developed, related to the students' growth and need by good student personnel procedures, and rounded out by the type of co-curricular experiences our communities can offer, is actually for the mature student a unique educational opportunity. Program development to provide such resources and the adequate interpretation needed to gain understanding for it are the greatest challenges we face.

---

[2] Arno J. Haack, "Student Life in an Urban University," at the annual meeting of the Association of Urban Universities, Detroit, October 27, 1952.

It is time to stop being apologetic for our differences and for the limitations of campus patterns that are more reminiscent of a romantic past than adequate as preparation for today's world.

It should be in our power to combine our potential assets to meet the needs of students in a unique way, thus serving them, and their communities through them, at an increasingly higher level.

Most students come to the municipal university campus without aggressive recruiting on the part of the institution. It is common to make the institution's facilities and programs well-known in the community and nearby area but only a few do much recruiting for students from a distance. As dormitory facilities are increased, more effort may be expected to be put into attracting the students who will live in them.

There is variation in policy as to whether the nonresident student should be required to meet higher entrance standards than the citizen of the local community. There is, however, no question but that the institution has the right to set whatever requirements it wishes for those who do not live in the area that supports the university by public funds.

Use of a junior college or lower division for a trial for the less likely student has enabled some municipal universities to raise the entrance requirements for their degree colleges, while still meeting the public expectation that a tax-supported university should give any high school graduate at least a chance to try it. This two-year proving ground has eased quite a bit of the pressure on the other divisions.

### Their Educational Heritage

It is the promise of American democracy that everyone may be educated to the limit of his ability or his desires. Recognition that talent does not belong to any particular class or society has long been a part of the democratic heritage and is now the dominant philosophy of education in the United States. It has meant a phenomenal increase in enrollment in institutions of higher education since 1900, when fewer than 250,000 students (only 4 per cent of the population 18 to 21 years of age) were registered. By 1950 enrollment had jumped to the unprecedented peak of 2,-

354,000 which included approximately one million veterans whose education was deferred because of World War II. There are predictions of staggering heights to which college enrollments will soar in the near future.

The rapid increase in enrollments has encouraged the belief that the United States is a country of college graduates. The growth of America's nationwide system of public universities, theoretically enabling almost any boy or girl to study for a college degree, has strengthened this belief. It is surprising, therefore, to hear from a former U.S. Commissioner of Education that there are at present two million young men and women in this country who deserve but cannot afford a higher education.

A study for the Commission on Financing Higher Education, published in 1952, indicates that only one out of every ten children in elementary school acquires a college degree. Of the students in the upper half of the high school graduating classes, only six out of ten plan to attend college full time. On the other hand, 30 per cent of the graduates in the lowest quarter of their high school graduating classes plan to attend college.

Many factors in addition to academic ability and achievement play a part in determining whether or not a high school graduate continues his education. These include the educational attainment of parents, the ambition of parents for their children's further education, the family's income and need for financial support from the children, the preference of some young people for obtaining jobs rather than continuing in school, the influence of adolescent friends upon each other, military service interfering with plans after high school graduation, and the kinds of jobs that happen to be available. The municipal university provides a set of conditions which make higher education more readily available. It might be well to note some of these briefly:

1. A higher percentage of high school graduates go to college in the city where there is a tax-supported university than where the institution is private. This is a matter of simple economics. Savings on room and board are the same, no matter what the nature of the institution, but the difference lies in tuition and similar fees.

2. Lower tuition and fees are available to city residents in return

for community support. This is the greatest encouragement for more young people to attend. As a corollary it might be mentioned that a growing enrollment then can become an argument for continued or increased tax or other financial aid.

3. The municipal university, because of its tax support, often is required to admit any graduate of its city high schools. This is encouraging to the youth who does not rank so well scholastically and might give only little thought to college if it means trying to hurdle the higher entrance requirements of a private college, no matter where it is located.

4. There is some tendency to plan to follow one's older friends to college, especially when the high school senior sees them frequently. He hears them talk about it at home, in social contacts, at church, in organizations. The youth about to be graduated from high school becomes interested in his friends' fraternity or other activities, and often has made some decision about a college affiliation. This situation is different when the older youth goes away for his education and may return only two or three times during the year. He has made a wide circle of new friends and most of the ties with the hometown crowd are cut.

5. The youth who holds a part-time job during high school does not need to decide between continuing the job or going to college. He can have both if he stays where he is. This financial aid may be required for sheer necessities, or it may enable him to avoid the dilemma of many a youth—college or car? He can have both in many cases; university parking lots are evidence of this. The same kind of choice is less pressing even in regard to marriage and parenthood. Again it is the closeness of a combination of job, parents, friends, and the educational institution.

## To Go or Not To Go

The following data are taken from a 1953 study[3] which the author directed of 10,830 high school graduates in New York who did not go to college. The findings indicate some reasons back of such an important decision.

---

[3] *Crucial Questions About Higher Education* (Albany, N.Y.: State University of New York, 1955).

The influence of young people upon each other may be one of the factors which helps them decide whether or not to continue. Of 4,508 who said they were interested in attending college, even though they did not do so, 33 per cent said most of their friends were continuing; of 5,547 who did not desire to attend college, only 17 per cent said most of their friends would do so. The study did not indicate that impending military service had any importance in shaping the decision to go or not to go to college.

That parents' educational experience affected plans of the children was shown by the fact that only 13 per cent of those not continuing beyond high school were children of fathers with some education beyond high school, and only about 5 per cent were children of college graduates. By contrast, among the youths continuing their education, 40 per cent had fathers who continued beyond high school and 24 per cent had fathers who were college graduates.

Of the 10,830 in the noncontinuing group, 5,773 reported that their parents wished them to continue. In this group 94 per cent of the boys and 82 per cent of the girls reported that their parents were interested in having them continue in school.

It is questionable whether young people know accurately the extent to which their families need the financial support which the son or daughter might provide. Nevertheless, 23 per cent of these 10,830 graduates stated that their financial support was required at home.

The differences in the income level of the groups surveyed are striking. The group attending four-year colleges contained six times as large a proportion of family incomes over $8,000 as the group who wanted to attend college but could not. This second group contained one and one-half times as large a proportion of family incomes under $4,000 as the first group.

Evident also was the contrast in income of young people attending two-year and four-year colleges, but the two-year college group comes from a higher economic level than students who did not go to college. This indicates the serious damage done to the ambitions of youth who desire higher education whenever the economic barrier is raised by increases in charges levied directly against students. The evidence suggests a need for lowering the economic barrier by providing more opportunities for students to attend college while living at home, by keeping tuition and fees low, and by providing more scholarship grants to students.

Graduates answered the question as to whether they would continue their education if they could afford to do so. Of 1,382 who said "yes" (all were acceptable potential students), 64 per cent reported family incomes under $4,000 and 34 per cent had incomes of between $4,000 and $7,999. Only 2 per cent had incomes of $8,000 or over.

What is the significance of these statistics for a municipal institution? It is that large numbers of students who have sufficient ability to pursue college studies are lost to the more highly educated portion of the manpower resources of the state and nation. Of the group surveyed in New York a large proportion were of superior academic ability.

The municipal university plays an important role in providing for the needs of these groups. The funds required to carry a student through his years of college will depend upon many factors. If he lives at home, for example, he will need less money than if he lives on a college campus. He must plan on many other items of cost such as books and supplies, clothes, laundry, transportation, amusement, recreation, social functions, health expenses, and personal items ranging from haircuts to postage stamps.

The major student charges are tuition and fees and room and board at college dormitories. The other items are more largely under a student's own control since they can be curtailed or expanded according to individual desire and resources. Such expenses, nevertheless, may amount to a substantial total. College students who live at home, which most do who attend municipal universities, will save mainly in amounts spent for room and board.

Armed with some knowledge of how much he will need to pay for his college education, the student then must consider the source of this money. Everyone will find it in a slightly different way because of varying individual circumstances. In general, however, a major source of funds for college expenses is the student's parents. In addition he can, in a varying degree, look to scholarships, loan funds, proceeds of insurance policies, accumulated savings, gifts, and (particularly in municipal universities) money which he himself can earn. The cash support given by most parents is nearly twice as much if a student lives on campus as if he lives at home. In theory at least, one of the reasons for awarding scholarships is to help students overcome economic barriers. Many organizations and private colleges which provide scholarships do take financial need into account. This is also true of municipal universities which have in recent years made a sustained effort to increase scholarship aid.

Scholarships do not solve all the problems. For example, there is the needy student who cannot attain the academic achievement expected of the scholarship holder, but if he has promise he may get financial assistance through a grant-in-aid. If this is not available, he can turn to borrowing. Borrowing money for educational costs, although common, has not been the preferred method, for it involves mortgaging the future. The National Defense Education Act, however, and numerous loan plans being developed by banks and other financial institutions have made this kind of financing much more attractive now.

Working for cash or for board or room or both is one of the means by which students help finance their college education. This is particularly true in campus schools. In municipal universities the students are able to spend part of their time in off-campus employment which will help to pay for tuition, books, and other necessary expenditures. Ordinarily, it is found that a larger percentage of those who live at home than those who live on campus work during the college year. Cash obtained from summer work and from work during the school year can be substantial.

The degree to which large family income bolsters college attendance makes even more significant the role of the municipal university. The boy or girl with low ability but relatively high family income has a better chance of planning a college career than does the youth in the highest ability bracket with a low family income. Indeed, family income exerts a greater influence about a decision to pursue higher education than does the ability of high school graduates as indicated by intelligence quotients, although both factors are important.

President Spathelf of Ferris Institute has said:

The student body of the modern urban university is the most heterogeneous to be found in the American collegiate scene. It mirrors accurately the melting pot structure of the modern metropolis because the university, accessible as it is, represents the accepted common denominator for individual betterment and personal achievement. The ditch-digger's son, the banker's daughter, the child of the immigrant, the product of the slum, the Negro lad, the aspiring self-made man—the list could be endless—comprise its totality. Economic selectivity and its resultant social selectivity have been reduced by the availability of educational opportunity and its relatively modest cost. . . .

. . . The normally accepted programs and service of and for students on the bucolic campus have their place in the urban campus for similar educational reasons. Differences become those of emphasis as the unique needs of the urban student body are met. To these, however, must be added innovations in practice for reason of the same uniqueness.[4]

## Religion in a Municipal University

One cannot consider the students in a municipal university without taking note of one of the items mentioned in the Michigan survey.[5] Nearly one out of five students was influenced in his choice of college because it was connected in some way with a "preferred group," usually denominational. This connection is something the tax-supported municipal university cannot offer its students. In this respect it is no different from other public universities; yet this should not give the impression that there is no concern for moral and spiritual development of the young men and women who attend.

The university's concern, however, is tempered by the fact that the local student has not been wrenched from either his church or his home when he enters upon his college career. Both continue to wield considerable influence. He retains his church membership, his same church friends, and his same church activities. The set pattern has some tendency to continue, but even under these circumstances many youths at college drift away from church.

---

4 Victor F. Spathelf, *Proceedings*, Thirty-Eighth Annual Meeting, Association of Urban Universities, 1952, p. 49.

5 Donald E. Wells, *Search* (East Lansing, Mich.: Michigan State University, 1961), Vol. 6, No. 2.

One of the paradoxes of this Christian nation founded on Christian principles is that religion is de-emphasized in the public schools and in the publicly supported institutions of higher learning. While the principle of separation of church and state is sound, in that it protects heterogeneous theological interests and prevents the domination of one over others, this principle often fosters neglect of religion as a whole.

It is true that specific religious beliefs should not be taught within the precincts of a public university. This concession is made because it would be impossible to consider all the shades of meaning and nuances of significance predicated by theological differences. Nevertheless, the religious spirit, mankind's passion to identify himself with a higher power, his conviction that his destiny is in the hands of an eternal deity—these have dominated, formed, and given direction to his greatest aspirations and achievements. Religion, indeed, is a perennial dimension of the life of man. All known human societies have sought some kind of adjustment with the Ultimate; and all have developed doctrines, rituals, and precepts to articulate their sense of dependence on a higher power.

One can hardly understand history, art, literature, philosophy, and social institutions without taking into account the influences of religion. In particular, the spirit of western civilization is intelligible only to one who realizes the extent to which concepts and values of the Judeo-Christian tradition permeate it.

In spite of this permeating emotional and spiritual influence, an overwhelming majority of students in municipal universities rarely have the opportunity to come to grips in any fundamental way with man's essential religious experiences and teachings. They pursue the complexities of politics, psychology, philosophy, music, art, and literature; but only accidentally do they make the acquaintance of masterpieces of religious literature. They come in contact with religious thinking only indirectly. The contacts are through the ideas of scholars, poets, artists, and philosophers deeply immersed in religious experiences. The emphasis is on the secular aspects of these great minds, not upon the spiritual influences from which they drew inspiration.

The student is encouraged to think on a high level about various secular subjects. Only rarely does it occur to him to reflect on religion at a comparable level; he seldom proceeds beyond the simple concepts of childhood. When religious experience is relegated to the infantile level, it is detrimental and ultimately leads to rejection. It is seldom considered that religion can be a strengthening, enlightening, and enriching experience throughout all of one's personal life. Treating it condescendingly destroys it; neglecting it in the field of higher education tends to render it contemptible. In the end the university contributes to its ineffectuality—a quality which many critics describe with scorn and continuously challenge theologians to explain. The universities are the destroyers who blame the destruction on the innocent. To be sure, it would not be fair to charge the universities with direct responsibility in this matter. They certainly have not intended to create an atmosphere foreign to religious growth. If they are culpable, it is through omission rather than commission. Unhappily, it must be said, universities indirectly foster the impression that religious considerations are not real. In consequence, the average student too often is influenced by the assumption that religion does not deserve the academic prestige accorded other fields. From this, it is but a step to the conclusion that with the educated—with those who know—religion does not count.

The greater number of young people today talk very little about religion. They remain silent, not because they are militantly resistant or atheistic—certainly not because they are indifferent—but simply because they are profoundly bewildered. They are bewildered because the church does not seem to speak their language and because, when religion does speak, its language seems to have lost its vitality and meaning.

Then, there is a confusion of a thousand different sects. By one recent count there are more than one thousand different Protestant sects in the United States. Is it strange, then, that youth is bewildered? Is it difficult to understand why universities cannot systematically teach religion? Should they try to bring an intelligible concept of religious faith to students, they probably would be stopped by any one of a number of conflicting theological interests.

Many college teachers and administrators see it this way: religion is a subject replete with controversy. There are too many different points of view, each with a heavy emotional investment. It is best, therefore, not to risk colliding with any of them. A municipal university—or any public institution, they feel—can neither condemn nor approve any particular set of religious teachings, and had best remain neutral. Only in this way will the municipal university continue to enjoy the freedom to pursue matters which are its proper concern without risking criticism or outside interference. Such criticism, they fear, might jeopardize the spirit of free inquiry, which is the university's very life.

The universities face, then, this dilemma: they may introduce religion into the curriculum and thereby risk incurring criticism or external pressure and intervention; or they may seek to avoid such dangers by ignoring religion, though overlooking many students' needs and wishes.

There is no need to despair, however. Municipal universities need not ignore religion because they cannot favor any particular religious teaching. Municipal universities do not dispense with the teaching of political philosophies because institutionally they cannot commit themselves to any particular party platform. Admittedly, religion and politics, improperly taught, can create difficulties and embarrassments. But in either case the dangers may be avoided, not by eliminating the courses, but by insuring that they are well-taught.

Courses in religion at a municipal university cannot be compulsory for all students, nor should they be. The courses should be available to students who desire them. They must be on a high academic level. There is a subject matter to be presented, and the teacher's function is to present it. His task is not to convert students to religion or away from it, but to provide them with a basis of understanding for making their own decisions.

It is often forgotten that some young people's most difficult adjustment problems center about religious orientation. Almost every college student has to do some rethinking on his religious principles in the light of new materials to which college introduces him. In almost every case, the student's difficulties arise because he is attempting to reconcile a religion learned as a child with the science he encounters as a young adult. The university cannot escape the responsibility of at least giving him the chance to acquire an understanding of religion on the same level with his understanding of science.

# CHAPTER VI

# The Non-Degree Student

There are those who believe the university should confine its attention to the full-time degree student, and who even are doubtful of the propriety of instructing the part-time student at night. Usually this view also holds that career-motivation in higher education is to be deplored, and certainly that specialized course work for employees on the job is not properly a university task.

This philosophy would take the university out of the main stream of American life. The educational needs of people transcend the neatly compartmentalized packages of curriculum planners. If we believe that education is central to individual growth and to the well-being of our civic and economic life, then the university, particularly the urban university, will make every effort to extend its resources to all who can benefit from them. It accepts community service as a main-line responsibility and seeks directly to fill community needs in many ways.[1]

## Education for the Many

A glance at enrollment statistics for municipal universities shows that the full-time student seeking a baccalaureate degree is in the minority; he is outnumbered by students in other categories. There are part-time students, evening students, non-degree students, graduate students, and those in all sorts of programs of less than the traditional length.

This diversity of the student body can give rise to concern about the quality of the institution as a whole. Purposes and goals of the programs vary; entrance standards are not alike, and in general the situation is quite foreign to that found in the closely-knit liberal arts college in the setting of a small community. Proper internal organization is necessary if each division in a complex university is to maintain its individuality, perform its own function, and avoid

---

[1] David D. Henry, in *Adult Education for Everybody* (New York: New York Adult Education Council, Inc., 1954). Copied from Association of Urban Universities *Newsletter,* May & June, 1959.

affecting the others adversely. The success with which the municipal universities continue to meet accreditation standards is an indication that this can be done and is being done. Adherence to a program which is too restricted would indicate lack of awareness or, even worse, indifference to the educational needs of the community.

That there is considerable demand for programs of two years or less is shown by the increase in junior or community colleges throughout the nation in recent years. Curriculums common to these have their place in the offerings of the municipal university. In many cases it is more practical that its services include such offerings than for the community to be forced into the added expense of setting up new institutions for this purpose. The tax-supported university hardly could escape this responsibility even if it wished to do so. Therefore it seems pertinent to take up the question of varied programs for a student body in which will be found differences in training, ability, goals, age, experience, interest, and motivation.

An advantage of two-year programs to a municipal institution is that these programs help meet the public demand that every high school graduate should have a chance to prove himself in college if he wishes.

In the baccalaureate colleges there is a real problem if the only admissions requirement is a high school diploma. Both teaching and learning can be difficult if a freshman class has too wide a range of aptitude for college-level work. It is expected that a high rate of attrition will be the result, and this is not necessarily productive of the best public attitude toward the institution.

The junior college gives an opportunity to the student who might meet difficulties in following a four-year curriculum. Far better for him to be in a program of shorter duration which he can complete successfully.

Some comments from an editorial in *The Blade* on the problem of raising educational standards in state-supported universities are applicable to the situation in municipal institutions as well. The writer states:

. . . there is an essential difference between public and private institutions; a presumptive right of all citizens to attend state-supported colleges and universities so long as they can actually do the required work.

No matter how much the state colleges and universities are permitted to select students, ultimately their standards will depend on what they require of students *after* they arrive on campus.

Admittedly, state schools are handicapped by freshman classes overloaded with poorly prepared students. Yet there is nothing in Ohio law barring state universities from separating students with good and weak high school records so that the better students will be challenged to their full capacity. . . .

However the state colleges and universities act to meet the needs of students with widely varying preparation, their primary obligation will not change. It is to insist upon high standards that will insure a meaningful education to any student willing and able to demonstrate his right to learn—by proving it in practice.[2]

The rising number of youths now filling the schools and aiming for college is a matter of nation-wide concern. The President's Committee on Education Beyond the High School, appointed to study the problem, opened its First Interim Report in 1956 with these words:

> The inescapable fact about the future of education beyond the high school is that in 1956 almost twice as many children will be born in the United States as were born in 1936. Already more people than ever before are attending the nation's colleges, universities and other post–high school educational institutions, yet the impact of the greatly increased birth rates of the past 15 years will shortly strike, and will be felt with mounting intensity each year as far into the future as we can foresee. Moreover, the patterns already emerging in our society will necessitate that a much higher percentage of this vastly increased population receive training after high school.

For most states there is general agreement on the magnitude of the coming problem. Barring a complete reversal of trends (and the evidence is the other way) it is certain that more young people will attend high school and will want and require education beyond that level.

The educational institution which is free to select its students is able to restrict enrollment to a top percentile of high school

---

[2] *The* [Toledo] *Blade,* June 16, 1961. Used by permission.

graduates and even exercise control over geographical distribution, the field of academic interest of the student, and the activities in which he is proficient. In other words, it is quite possible to have a "tailor-made" student body. This naturally makes for a different kind of college or university from one where tax support makes necessary a much more liberal admissions policy.

Faculty members sometimes envy the college which accepts students from only, say, the top 25 per cent of the high school graduates. An array of such potential talent is a real stimulus to the good teacher. But what about the other 75 per cent? These young people have talents, too. Some are bountifully blessed, but perhaps not so broadly as their fellows who make A's in every subject. Some have lesser talent in more restricted fields.

Has a public institution the right to slam the door in the belief that there are too many who are uneducable to make it worth while bothering with them, the bottom third for example? Education for excellence does not necessarily mean that college should be restricted only to those who have made excellent records in high school. Education for excellence can mean the job of giving many young men and women the opportunity to improve themselves for citizenship, for a career, and for living useful lives enriched by college experience.

If this nation concentrates upon the top quartile, this intellectual elite can provide fine leadership, but it still is the other three-fourths who will produce most of the nation's goods, buy most of its products, pay most of the taxes, elect officials, and in the long run determine national policies at the polls. Who can deny that as much education as possible is just as important for them as it is for those who are training to enter the professions?

The question a municipal university faces is: what institutional arrangements should it be making to accommodate a great influx of students in the near future? The extent to which private colleges and other public universities may move to meet part of the problem is a separate and important issue. It should not detract from prior thoughtful consideration of the direction a municipal university should take in caring for what must be a substantial portion of the coming student body. Decisions on the matter must show a consistent regard for the proper and most desirable education of the students, and the organization's own inherent quality as a university.

## General Education

The two-year programs which meet a part of this demand must take into account the need for both technical education and that of a more general nature. Technical education already has achieved recognition for its role in training beyond the high school. Institutes for such education long since have been established in many states. It is particularly true that the technical programs meet a need which is much more dramatic and capable of being much more graphically portrayed than is the case with the general education programs. Yet, the answer must be an unequivocal "no" to the question of whether the nation can rely on technical programs alone to meet the demand of larger numbers of high school graduates. This solution is undesirable practically and intellectually. Specialized programs are costly. They require extensive equipment, which in many cases must be replaced frequently because it is consumed or because it becomes obsolete. The teaching staff for such programs is hard to find and frequently is expensive because of competition from industry.

Such a solution is intellectually undesirable because what adults in general need is a broad flexible base upon which they can build lives as members of families and as citizens as well as workers. As the California Restudy states it:

> Individuals are not workers alone, but also citizens, members of families and other social groups, and persons with special interests and needs. Numerous studies have shown that many beginning workers are unsuccessful on the job, not because they lack technical training, but because they are unable to adjust to their fellow employees or to cope with the nonvocational aspects of their living.

Furthermore, a highly specialized program requires a young person to commit himself at an earlier age than may be desirable for him or for society. Many students do not understand themselves well enough to decide at an early age to devote a lifetime to a certain technical pursuit. An institutional arrangement which forces them to do so often produces incompetent and unhappy adults.

The intellectual undesirability of early commitment to specialized training is eloquently stated by Woodrow Wilson in his address on the ideal university:

> The average thoughtful American does not want his son narrowed in all his gifts and thinking to a particular occupation . . . He desires a training for him which will give him a considerable degree of elasticity and adaptability, and fit him to turn in any direction he chooses. For men do not live in ruts in America . . . Versatility, adaptability, a wide range of powers, a quick and easy variation of careers, men excelling in businesses for which they never had any special preparation,—these are among the most characteristic marks of American life.[3]

What then is the solution to this very large problem? More technical programs would contribute only a partial solution for the hundreds of young men and women who would be seeking education beyond the secondary school.

Sound programs of general education are not only in the best interests of the two-year colleges, but of the four-year colleges as well. Within the four-year colleges, an increasing trend toward specialization, together with the excesses of the unbridled elective system, have resulted in a fragmentation of the curriculum. In this fashion, the liberal arts colleges have tended to abandon their traditional responsibility for liberal education. A common, profoundly conceived core of general education in two-year colleges would help to restore the four-year college to its proper function and would serve excellently for those students for whom it may be terminal.

The general programs of the two-year college will serve admirably the needs of those adults who wish to broaden their understanding, but who, for one reason or another, have never finished high school. Many such adults, matured by their experience, are capable and interested in a stimulating general education program and should not be excluded because of formal requirements. In this way the city can discharge its obligation to its older citizens as well, and its youth will have first-hand experience with the continuing vitality and importance of education.

---

[3] Ray Stannard Baker and William E. Dood, eds., *Public Papers of Woodrow Wilson,* Part One, *College and State* (New York: Harper & Brothers, 1925), Vol. 2, pp. 147–159.

In serving their function of providing education for great numbers of students, municipal universities appropriately should maintain modest entrance standards. No normal man is uneducable and all are or will be citizens. The city profits by the improved intelligence of all its electorate. Varying the standards of admission does not necessarily result in an inferior program. There can be good programs for average students just as there can be superior programs for superior students. These programs will require all the ingenuity of the faculty, whose art will be truly exercised in the process of providing top-level programs stimulating for both average and exceptional students.

Difficulty can be anticipated in finding a faculty capable of devising a sound general education program that is both terminal and continuing. Teachers, however, can be found who are interested in general education and who see in this honorable career a challenge deserving their best talents. The developing of broad critical powers in students can be as exciting as the developing of highly trained specialists.

The enormous growth of new knowledge and techniques in the highly industrialized modern world has led understandably to the development of numerous specialized schools. As the trustees of the Carnegie Foundation for the Advancement of Teaching stated in their 1955–56 annual report: "Such specialist education is essential to our national life, but higher education will suffer an irreparable loss if it neglects those other portions of the curriculum that place the man before the occupation." Broad educational programs must be provided in colleges which can successfully resist the pressures for excessive fragmentation. There must be sound basic programs in the natural sciences, the social sciences, and the humanities which carefully preserve the identity of each and their interrelationship. Upon such a foundation, more specialized programs can be built to meet the particular needs and interests of the student while preserving an essential connection with the other fields of knowledge.

## Weighing the Programs

Yet, with the increased emphasis on two-year colleges, there is need to appraise the degree of their public acceptance, particularly those which are terminal in nature. This is an important factor in planning. It cannot be assumed that large numbers of students can be diverted into appropriate two-year programs if they are not ready to accept the two-year college as adequate for their needs and their prestige. Public opinion generally favors support of twelve grades at public expense. When grades 13 and 14 become acceptable as a necessity, two more years will be added to the program. Much of this, incidentally, will have to be done as a public undertaking by and for the benefit of the people as a whole.

Furthermore, there is need to consider what kind of guidance young people are getting and will receive in the future in respect to two-year, technical terminal education and in certain other areas where the level of prestige is not so high, but where the need for product is much greater. Two-year programs do not appear to be as "respectable" as those for four years. Are the students receiving unprejudiced counsel on their future? Many young people who were steered into four-year curriculums might better have entered a two-year program.

There is need for better statistics on the ability of youth entering four-year programs and on the drop-out rate of college students. Some of the available information on drop-outs makes depressing reading and raises the broad question of what colleges and universities are trying to accomplish with the students who are now enrolled, as well as the collective needs of the society which provides that higher education and to which the students eventually will return. Clearly no well-conceived purpose is being accomplished for a large number of presumably qualified students who fail to complete successfully the courses they have begun.

What are the causes of this failure? Is it the sterility of the program that causes good students to leave college? Is it the teaching? Is it finances? It may be argued that drop-outs are not of college caliber. If so, then it may be relevant to state that the universities are guilty of a disservice when they admit young men and women who are not qualified to do college work.

There is need for more adequate information on the kinds and amounts of abilities required in different occupational and professional fields. Do the educational programs—and the requirements thereof—take into account the kinds and amounts of abilities required? What is the relationship, if any, between the kinds and amounts of abilities required for different occupational fields and the academic programs that prepare for these fields? If an orderly process of education is to prevail, abilities required in occupations must be cataloged; programs for their development must be consistent; and students must be selected who have the greatest promise of success.

There is need to know more about what higher education facilities will be necessary to obtain the most effective development of the nation's manpower resources. The quality of its manpower is the nation's principal asset; it must have optimum quality development to compete with those countries which have many more men available. What percentages of increase in various professional and technical fields are indicated? What are the implications of translating such manpower needs into college and technical school enrollments? The significance of such projections becomes apparent when it is noted that in 1950 college administrators were being warned by an agency of the Federal Government that the colleges were turning out too many engineers.

Can more be learned about the factors that prevent young people with superior ability from continuing their education beyond the high school? Nearly a fifth of superior high school graduates do not plan further education. Since it is known that finances are not the only factor, steps should be taken to find out why such potentially fine professional people are virtually lost to the highest potential segment of the manpower resources. What motivation is necessary to obtain more adequate development of these young people?

Along with all these questions should go a basic attitude: one of receptiveness to change, one which is astatic by nature and flexible in operation. Educators need constantly to re-examine their basic premises. Is there any practice or policy in higher education which is sacrosanct? Certainly not—and educators should prove their receptiveness to new ideas by challenging all the old ideas that get in the way of flexible operation. This extends all the way from the structure of college buildings to the size of the faculty, the teaching load, the length of the university's working day, and the credit hours in some curriculum.

## Continuing Education

Now, what about those students who are older than the average college age? Night classes filled with men and women of all ages and from all walks of life have flourished for years in urban institutions. That the opportunity to attend college is beneficial to them is unquestioned, whether the individual's goal may be improvement on his job, preparation for a better one, pursuit of a personal interest, the desire for knowledge for its own sake, social prestige, a degree, mere curiosity, or sheer avoidance of boredom or loneliness.

Educational opportunity at a municipal university is not a "one-shot" affair to be taken on a full-time basis right after high school or not at all. A municipal university offers continuing post-high school education to all who are interested and able, irrespective of age.

Interest in adult education has continued over a long period. It was in 1919 that Frederick B. Robinson, who later became president of the City College of New York, said:

> The educator cannot well adhere to the Chinese tradition and content himself with passing on the wisdom and information of the past. He must also be an active agent in the life of the present and a strong influence in shaping progress; he must be a co-ordinator and a manipulator of action and reaction between the individual and his physical and social environment to the end that the whole social mass will enjoy increased well being. He finds his greatest opportunity in the field of urban, adult education.

Robinson's comments, made at a meeting of the Association of Urban Universities in Boston, might have been uttered only yesterday. Diversity is the keynote. Some adults who attend evening classes take the same degree programs pursued by students in the day sessions. Others enroll in programs which are suitable for their own needs. The executive-development program is an example of one area of adult education that has become increasingly important. Industries throughout the country have recognized the desirability of giving broader background and perspective to their middle management personnel from whom tomorrow's top management will be drawn. Enrollment in these programs is limited to persons offered the opportunity by their employer who, incidentally, pays the full cost for a class which is not open to the public. Since these programs can be given during evening hours, it is not necessary for local industries to lose the services of their executives temporarily, as would be required by a program at an out-of-town institution.

The preparation of separate course sequences for individuals is a different type of adult education. For example, the salesman who finds he needs some technical knowledge consults with a university staff member to find a sequence of courses that will help him perform his work better.

In other words, the urban university provides the opportunity for local citizens to keep growing in their occupations and relate their education to their experience and prospective advancement. It is not necessary to lose time from the job, and there is no out-of-town travel required.

Special interest courses for adults cover a wide variety of cultural, civic, and technical subjects. These are non-credit offerings pinpointed toward a particular community interest. Some of them need only be given once; some are added to the offerings of other adult centers in the community; some may develop eventually into college credit courses and find their way into the requirements of programs leading to degrees. The following list shows their range: taxation problems of small business, club clinic for club women, popular astronomy, a century of ideas in plays and playwrights, psychology in everyday living, industrial inspection, applications of automatic controls, industrial quality control, or beginning Italian.

The point can be made without further detail or elaboration, for adult education has been treated quite fully in a growing volume of literature. In the round-the-year programs of any urban university, the needs of this group will be recognized. In the municipally supported institution this is particularly true, for this kind of institution feels even more strongly its obligation for service to meet the needs of individual citizens and the broader needs of the community as a whole.

Yet a word of warning is needed. It is voiced by Donald Z.

Woods, Dean of the College of Adult Education of the Municipal University of Omaha, who states:

> The University of Omaha is an urban, municipal university with a specified area of a few square miles in which to work. Within this area—and mindful that we cannot be all things to all people—we endeavor to determine what is, or will become, a specific need in the community, sometimes before the community is aware a need exists or threatens, and attempt to respond to the best of our ability, through education. While we have many side concerns, our main concentration is a positive approach in proving to the community that we are doing more for each tax dollar than, in our opinion, anyone else could do . . . To serve the wide range of community interests, a municipal university must know its aims and purposes and where to draw the line.[4]

---

[4] From the Conference on the Role of the University in an Urban Setting, University of Wisconsin-Milwaukee, October 29, 1960.

## CHAPTER VII

# The Municipal University
# and the Press

The administrator does not operate in a social and economic vacuum. There is always political handwriting on the wall for him to read, and it does no good to turn his back and say, "We are not as other men are." Sooner or later he will discover that the American university is a public university and that the citizen and his agents have the whip hand. The university is not for the professors, or the president, or even for the student. It is for the people. This is as it should be in a democracy.[1]

### Spotlight on the Campus

Whether a municipal university meets the responsibility it bears in return for the support it receives from the people of its community is a matter of public concern. Certainly there is no lack of interest among citizens. It is to be expected, then, that a municipal university will find itself under close surveillance by the press, which naturally is concerned with the public interest. This need not be considered an undesirable situation, although at times it can be an uncomfortable one.

Many administrators are under the impression that they live in a goldfish bowl, but it is interesting to find that there is not unanimous agreement on this point. Former Senator William Benton is reported to have said in an address before the American Conference of Academic Deans: "One weakness of our colleges on which you may not agree is the absence of informed, systematic, outside criticism." He asked, "Who is helping the college bridge the tremendous gap between what it does and what it says it does; who is helping with criticism so that it has a better chance to do what it wants to do?"

---

[1] Clarence A. Schoenfeld, *The University and Its Publics* (New York: Harper & Brothers, 1954), p. 180.

From the quotation it is uncertain whether Mr. Benton was being more critical of the colleges or the press. Few municipal university administrators would be likely to complain that the press had been lacking interest or negligent in expressing its views. However, they would have much more occasion to worry if the news media ignored them. This does not appear to be much of a possibility, for, as Eric Sevaried pointed out:

> . . . the local college or university in a great number of cities is becoming the central, the dominant and characterizing aspect of the community's life . . . Never before has the "downtown press" paid such informed and imaginative attention to the local classroom and laboratory as a rich source of exciting "hard" news. The college is no longer simply a traditional, respectable adornment for occasions of official local pride and chamber of commerce brochures.
>
> The colleges have entered into the daily life of the cities and states and they into the daily life of the colleges in a degree remarkable to one whose memories of college life were fashioned in the thirties.[2]

Journalistic scrutiny of the campus is based on the consideration that here is an important source of news interesting to the community at large. The education reporter can find plenty of material if he has the training and background to recognize it. It has been pointed out that many a significant event does not become news because newsmen fail to define the event as news. This is one of the reasons the press should not be too critical of publicity men on university staffs. One of their jobs is to call the attention of the press to news which might otherwise be overlooked in the spate of events. Education in the big city is big business—too big for one education editor or reporter to cover with any degree of thoroughness. If one wished to make comparisons, he might contrast the size of the newspaper sports department with that of the education department: 10 to 1, 20 to 1, or sometimes an even greater disparity.

Differences in ideas about the basic philosophy of education may be a source of some friction between the press and the local institution. The long-standing debate about liberal education and professional or vocational training is an example.

---

[2] Eric Sevaried, *The* [Toledo] *Blade,* February 26, 1961. Used by permission of the Hall Syndicate, Inc. All rights reserved.

The municipal university is under many pressures, too, and the manner in which it responds to these can become a subject for editorial comment, favorable or unfavorable. This can involve such matters as academic freedom, administrative shake-ups, development of new curriculums, control of students, how money is spent, and athletic programs.

The press sees policies and decisions being made at the board level, for open board meetings are expected, and rightly so. The presence of reporters at such meetings, especially if the same ones are assigned for some period of time, enables the representatives of the press to become well-acquainted with the institution and its problems. This can help promote amicable relations between the press and the administrator. A reporter who is well-informed should be capable of discussing university affairs freely with the president and at times he may be in a position to give the president some valuable advice if their rapport is good. Anything other than an open-door policy is difficult to justify in the relations between the president and representatives of the media of mass communication, and rather than fret about it, the educator should find means of making the best use of it.

The local press takes a paternal interest in the student newspaper, too. At the University of Toledo several years ago the student editor was dunked in the creek by some of his fellows who objected to some editorial comments. Naturally he immediately gained considerable local and even state-wide fame as a martyr, in a small way, to the principle of freedom of the press. The policy on the Toledo campus always has been one of editorial freedom and responsibility rather than close rein by faculty or administration. Proximity to the daily press of the city has been responsible for this, in part, and this has been true in other universities as well.

Financial facts of life are of public interest, since the taxpayer supplies some of the funds for the municipal institution. Again, in a relatively compact community there is news value in the income and cost of running a university which the citizens consider their own. One must expect articles, then, on budgets, salaries, boosts in students' fees, and similar financial matters.

In the case of a state university it may be that the legislature has the primary financial interest, but in a city, especially where the support comes directly from taxation, it is the individual citizen who expects to be kept informed on how his money is being used.

Any and all of these matters are likely to get rather thorough coverage—perhaps because, after all, three fourths or more of the students may come from homes within the newspaper's circulation zone or the radio or TV station's listening area. This comes close to saturation, a condition which can give the institution quick communication with the bulk of its constituents.

### Reciprocal Benefits

Both the press and the administrators of a municipal university should give some thought to the many ways in which their interests and activities are intertwined. Mutual recognition of these facts can help in promoting good relations between these two institutions.

The editor or publishers, first of all, should recognize that the university benefits the mass media by helping raise the standard of living. College-trained people are producers of wealth and consumers of products. Survey after survey has shown the higher earning power of this group. They drink more milk, use more telephones, buy more insurance, books, and newspapers. It also means in many cities more payroll taxes for community betterment and certainly a growing group of potential customers for advertisers.

In the second place, higher education provides the newspaper with a more alert reading audience. Again, surveys show that the better educated citizens not only read more newspapers but read them more thoroughly and critically. It is from this group the editor may expect to find many who are interested in something beyond the froth of the day's news. The university's principal contribution should be intellectual, and the press in the communities served by municipal universities looks upon this as important.

Third, the university provides manpower for every medium of communication—young men and women with promise of capabilities in writing, advertising, management, and other fields. College has at least screened out the less able, and has given its graduates some background and often technical training, so they will require a shorter period of apprenticeship once they are in the field. Universities do not claim to turn out ready-made experts, but they do expect to produce some potential experts who have been over the preliminary hurdles.

Education, then, provides much solid news. The municipal university is in the serious business of educating the nation's youth. There is significant news in the development of new ideas, educational philosophy, curriculum, programs, or research. The fringe activities on any campus seem to get plenty of space, even if they are not truly significant. Young people are always interesting, whether one follows them in sports, social activities, experiments in student government, or student elections.

There is a final consideration about the contribution of higher education to the press: the municipal colleges can and should serve a critical function. This is not necessarily a way to gain popularity with the press, but even the press will admit that somebody should do this job. How else is there likely to be improvement? The more astute members of the press will admit there is room for improvement in news analysis, as there is room for improvement in higher education. So far self-criticism by the press has not proved too stimulating to better performance, just as self-criticism in higher education has not always led to necessary reforms.

The press can do much for higher education, too. First, one of its functions is that of educating. The daily press is the people's college. It gives them a view of the worlds of science, civic affairs, international events, government, finance, arts, and music. It continues the educational function beyond the years of formal schooling and can stimulate the realization of the growing need for knowledge. Many persons, young and old, have been inspired to go or to return to college because of influence exerted by the mass media. It is difficult to estimate the tremendous educational influence of the press.

Second, in municipalities where there is a university the press protects the interests of higher education through its watchdog function. Just as the press will give a better performance if subject to intelligent criticism, so do the colleges and universities. Municipal universities find it to their advantage to welcome close scrutiny, for it serves as a cure for complacency and is a goad to progress. Informed and thoughtful editorial comment on issues involving education is not only good for the public but is good for education.

Third, the press helps the municipal university by publicizing its progress, people, and problems. Public understanding and support are so important that a municipal university must depend upon this method to get information to the greatest number of people in the shortest time. It would be far more difficult, if not impossible, and certainly far more expensive to do it any other way.

As a fourth contribution the daily press serves as a model for college newspapers. Such models can be either good or bad. It might give some newspapermen pause to realize that their product may help some young staffer decide whether journalism is to be the career for him or only an interesting college activity.

Finally, the press presents the university with a new text daily. It may be used in any one of a dozen areas—sociology, psychology, science, marketing, history, government, economics, English, journalism and others. The press supplements the printed matter which comes in textbooks, some already out of date by the time they are off the press. The reporter, knowing of this, finds it stimulating to be writing for college students and professors, who expect accuracy and a fair presentation in the material prepared for them every day.

## Joint Responsibilities

There are some joint responsibilities which should be recognized. The stake of the municipal university in the economic welfare of the city that supports it is obvious. For any medium of mass communication prosperity means more opportunity for the sale of advertising or copies of a publication. Prosperity means more tax income which in turn should mean public improvements, better recreational facilities for citizens, and better schools from kindergarten to college. For the university it means a better chance of financial support, whether it be from the city itself, business, industry, or individuals. It means that fewer able young people will have to pass up college for financial reasons. Both the press and higher education have an obligation to contribute something to the material progress of the community, if they wish to enjoy its fruits.

Each would find it difficult or impossible to exist without public support. It takes at least two things to gain this: the first is good performance, and the second is that this striving for excellence must be made known. The public as a whole is not likely to appreciate a job being done well unless it is called to its attention in some fashion.

Mention has been made that the press and higher education are alike in that each by the nature of its function will always be subject to public criticism. There never is unanimous applause for any action in the controversial areas of journalism and education. While the universities find it essential to be in the public eye, they recognize that there will be brickbats as well as bouquets. Perhaps part of the job of both journalism and education is to keep score for each other on the proportion of each kind of reaction. Journalists and educators find that they are subject to continuous and public scrutiny, not always friendly. Some of the time educators and editors feel they deserve a more sympathetic public attitude than they get, for it is always open season on them.

Newspapers traditionally have been in the position of a quasi-public utility with educational and public service functions as well as commercial ones. Without intense public interest the newspaper and the radio or TV station would find it hard to exist. Yet this attention leaves the way open for the critics to find material from which to dissent. Educators and editors are in a situation comparable to that of the football coach—there is never any lack of advice from those who are sure they could do the job better. It seems that nearly everyone is trying to say what is wrong with TV, radio, the newspapers, and education. In recent years the spotlight has been turned on colleges and universities. Municipally supported institutions have always operated under this glare, but the denominational and other private colleges are finding the same beam focused on them. After all, every college has a large part of the population interested in its affairs and, in this sense, all are public.

If educators are beleaguered at times by a hostile public, it may be due to a breakdown in communication between the college and the press, but queries of other municipal universities indicate that, in general, relations with the mass media are satisfactory. Open board meetings help promote this rapport, although it is not unusual for a newspaper to rely upon reports prepared by the institution's public relations or information office, even for such an important event as a board session.

One term which appears frequently in answers to questions about this matter is "constructive attitude." This would indicate that presidents of these institutions feel that even when there is criticism in the press it is given in an attempt to be helpful.

One might venture a guess that coverage of athletic events will raise more blood pressure than articles about any other topic. Sports fans, and often coaches, are inclined to read between the lines, to measure size of headlines jealously, or to take offense at expression of opinions which differ from their own. They say most sports are games of mere inches, and one is inclined to agree when he hears a rabid fan's cries of dismay if the opposing team gets two more column-inches of space than his own.

There are indications that administrators and reporters do not always see eye to eye as to what news is. For example, the comment that there is difficulty getting coverage of important events from time to time is not an unusual complaint, nor should it be too disturbing. It is the same comment which comes from all kinds of news sources involved in the competition for the limited space or time at the disposal of any medium of mass communication.

Newspapers, radio and television, and educational institutions that exist side by side recognize the need for answers to some significant questions.

Whose responsibility is it to see that the average citizen is well-informed on the status of education? Who should meet the assaults on the educational system from those who are probably well-intentioned but misinformed? How can a discussion of educational problems be presented on a somewhat higher plane than the mere protests that "the schools aren't what they were when I was a boy," or that "Johnny isn't learning to read"? Who understands the history and development of education and where it ought to be ten years hence? How much information does the average citizen have on the problem of future enrollments about which so much is heard? Does he know whether the college which has his interest has a good enough faculty, whether it is meeting with success in efforts to get and hold able teachers? Does he have any knowledge of the college plant other than the exterior view of gloomy red brick or shiny glass walls as he drives by? Does he know whether he casts his vote for the youth or the chancellor of the exchequer?

If the citizenry is to be informed on the importance of higher education today, on its value to the city and nation, and on every individual's personal stake in it, then the responsibility must be shared jointly by higher education and the press. Nowhere is this more true than in the community where there is close relationship between the people and their own university.

# CHAPTER VIII

# The Future of
# the Municipal University

If the university of the twentieth century is to have that place of leadership in our age held by our institutions of learning in the eighteenth and nineteenth centuries, it must . . . be located among the people, seeking to clear their vision, to gird them for new tasks, and to enrich and nourish their lives. The municipal university is, therefore, natural and inevitable; its rise marks an era in the development of American education second only to the founding of the public school in the eighteenth century and the opening of the state university in the nineteenth century.[1]

A half century ago there was no doubt in many minds about the future of the municipal university. It seemed destined to an ever-enlarging role, but more recently the pattern of higher education has shifted, and the outlook is not necessarily as it was when the Association of Urban Universities was just getting under way.

Is the municipal university a transitional or a permanent element in the American system of higher education? It came into being in response to local needs which no other agency was able or willing to meet. In general, municipal universities date back to a period when educational do-it-yourself was more popular, or at least more necessary. In a number of cases a community assumed the burden rather than suffer the total loss of a struggling institution. In others it was the case of meeting a need which, at that time, could be met in no other way.

Currently, and even more in the future, it is necessary that educational financing come from a wide base. The city itself is too restricted an area, with too many demands for increasingly costly services, to cause local law-makers and taxpayers to look with favor

---

[1] Lemuel H. Murlin, "Results of Cooperation by the Municipality and the University in Training for Public Service." Proceedings of the Annual Meetings of the AUU, 1914–15, p. 51.

upon soaring expenditures for higher education. Better to let the state or some other agency bear, or at least share, the cost. In most cities adequate financing of public schools through grade twelve requires relentless effort. Citizens understand that this is the first educational responsibility of the community. In some cases it becomes possible to finance two additional years, especially if this requires no new buildings and little in the way of administrative costs. The present school board and administration can handle most of the details. If much of the instruction is overtime work for teachers already in the system, instructional costs are quite low in contrast to those at an institution where the teaching is done by a full time faculty; but two years seems about the limit even in communities where the situation is most favorable.

All this would make it appear doubtful that any full-fledged four-year institutions, municipally supported, may be expected to appear in the future. The money, needed for so many other purposes, is not available. True, there seems to be a great desire on the part of some two-year community colleges to become four-year colleges. But this yearning, if realistic, has to be contingent upon support from the state, not a restricted local base.

If, then, the number of municipal universities is unlikely to increase, what about the future of those now in operation? Interestingly enough, the view is not gloomy although the picture will be changing. They seem destined to continue to provide strong educational leadership in their communities, which in turn appear able to maintain their present level of support. Whether this level can be expected to rise is doubtful, but even present sums provide a substantial financial backlog. Each assured million dollars a year, for example, is equivalent to the interest on an endowment of $25,000,-000 returning 4 per cent.

Local pride and a feeling of local need are factors which will tend to keep the municipal university in operation. A plank advocating abolition of a municipal institution would hardly help a political candidate get himself elected to office. In most cases this would mean little or no financial benefit to the city government, for if an institution's income is through a millage in the city charter it cannot be diverted to any other purpose. The only selling point for such an action would be that it would reduce taxes by a mill or two.

It is not quite realistic to discuss actual abolition of an institution of higher learning which serves the population of a metropolitan area. Business and industry have too much of a stake in it as a source of manpower, in-service training, or research. Parents, viewing rising college costs, turn to the local institution to help meet the expense of educating their children. For these and other reasons which have been apparent in this general discussion, the university in a city is a vital part of it, something it cannot afford to lose.

Rather, the question is: what changes in the pattern of support are likely to occur in the future? Led by university officials themselves, the community will press for additional financing from wider areas such as the county and metropolitan region or the state—in return for educational services rendered. It is not unlikely that for some a pattern of one-third from the student, one-third from local sources, and one-third from the state might prove practical. This will maintain some of the local autonomy and does not involve the twinge to local pride which might come from "giving the university to the state." But for others, even this may be transitional. The story of Wayne State University, for example, runs the gamut from city support to county-wide support to partial state assistance and finally to full status as a state university. It may be expected that this pattern will be repeated elsewhere.

Diekhoff, noting the change to a new trend, expressed some concern. He wrote:

> City colleges do not generally fully exploit the advantages of their kind, and communities do not fully exploit their colleges. Local colleges do not always recognize the advantages of their localism . . . If the local public colleges do not themselves develop an awareness of their own importance, if they do not learn to exploit their advantages and minimize their disadvantages, if the people of their communities do not insist upon retaining what is their own, the loss to our democracy will be great.[2]

The ranks of municipal universities have dwindled, but the remaining institutions continue to increase in size and service to ever-widening areas. It can be predicted that they will continue to seek new sources of support which will result in still broader service.

---

[2] John S. Diekhoff, *Democracy's College* (New York: Harper & Brothers, 1950), p. 36.

Most of them will hope to retain their identity, both for sentimental and practical reasons, but the changes sure to come may necessitate either a redefinition of the term "municipal university," or perhaps even lead to its disappearance as one of the categories in higher education.

# Bibliography

American College Public Relations Association, *The Advancement of Understanding and Support of Higher Education.* Washington, D.C.: The Association, 1958.

American Council on Education, *American Universities and Colleges.* Eighth ed. Washington, D.C.: The Council, 1960.

——, *Higher Education and the Society It Serves.* Washington, D.C.: The Council, 1957.

Association of University Evening Colleges, *Twentieth Annual Meeting, 1958.* New York: The Association, 1958.

Association of Urban Universities, *Newsletter.* Detroit: The Association, 1949– .

——, *Summary of Proceedings, Annual Meetings.* Detroit: The Association, 1927– .

Auburn, Norman P., *Report of the President, 1960–61.* Akron: The University of Akron, 1962.

Berelson, Bernard R., *Graduate Education in the United States.* New York: McGraw-Hill Book Co., Inc., 1960.

Boroff, David, *Campus U.S.A.* New York: Harper & Brothers, 1961.

Brownell, Baker, *The College and the Community; A Critical Study of Higher Education.* New York: Harper & Brothers, 1952.

Brubacher, John S. and Willis Rudy, *Higher Education in Transition.* New York: Harper & Brothers, 1958.

Carey, James T., *The Development of the University Evening College; As Observed in 10 Urban Universities.* Chicago: Center for the Study of Liberal Education for Adults, 1961.

——, *Forms and Forces in University Adult Education.* Chicago: Center for the Study of Liberal Education for Adults, 1961.

Carmichael, Oliver C., *Graduate Education; a Critique and a Program.* New York: Harper & Brothers, 1961.

——, *Universities: Commonwealth and American. A Comparative Study.* New York: Harper & Brothers, 1959.

Catalogs, College and University
Akron, The University of, *1961–62 Catalog.*
Brooklyn College, *Bulletin 1960–61.* XXX, No. 1, 1960.
Cincinnati, University of, *Annual Catalog of All Colleges 1961–1962.* Bulletin LVII, No. 16.
City College of New York, *Bernard M. Baruch School of Business and Public Administration, 1960–1961.*
Hunter College, *Bulletin, College of Arts and Sciences 1960–1961.* Sixtieth Series, No. 4, 1960.
Louisville, University of, *Bulletin of University of Louisville, College of Arts and Sciences.* LI, No. 1, 1957.

Newark College of Engineering, *Undergraduate Day and Evening Courses 1962–1963*.

Omaha, University of, *General Catalog 1959–1960—1960–61*. XX, No. 1.

Queens College, *General Catalog 1960–1961*. New York: Bulletin No. 24.

Toledo, The University of, *Bulletin of the College of Arts and Sciences*. XXXIX, No. 4, 1962.

Washburn University of Topeka, *Catalog 1960–1961*.

Wichita, University of, *Biennial Catalog, 1961–1962—1962–1963*. Bulletin XXVI, No. 3.

Chambers, Meritt Madison, *The Campus and the People: Organization, Support and Control of Higher Education in the U.S. in the Nineteen Sixties*. Danville, Ill.: The Interstate Printers and Publishers, Inc., 1960.

Commission on Financing Higher Education, *Nature and Needs of Higher Education*. New York: Columbia University Press, 1952.

Corson, John J., *Governance of Colleges and Universities*. The Carnegie Series in American Education. New York: McGraw-Hill Book Co., Inc., 1960.

DeVane, William Clyde, *The American University in the Twentieth Century*. Baton Rouge: Louisiana State University Press, 1957.

Diekhoff, John S., *Democracy's College*. New York: Harper & Brothers, 1950.

Eddy, Edward D., Jr., *Colleges for Our Land and Time*. New York: Harper & Brothers, 1957.

———, *The College Influence on Student Character*. Washington, D.C.: American Council on Education, 1959.

Educational Policies Commission, *Higher Education in a Decade of Decision*. Washington, D.C., 1957.

*The Educational Record*, XXXIX, No. 3, July, 1958.

Frankel, Charles, ed., *Issues in University Education*. New York: Harper & Brothers, 1959.

Gardner, John W., *Excellence*. New York: Harper & Brothers, 1961.

Glenny, L. A., *Autonomy of Public Colleges: The Challenge of Coordination*. New York: McGraw-Hill Book Co., Inc., 1959.

Harris, Seymour Edwin, et al., eds., *Higher Education in the United States; The Economic Problems*. Cambridge: Harvard University Press, 1960.

Harvard Student Council, *Religion at Harvard*. Cambridge: Harvard Student Council, 1956.

Havighurst, Robert J., *American Higher Education in the 1960's*. Columbus, Ohio: Ohio State University Press, 1960.

Henderson, Algo D., *Policies and Practices in Higher Education*. New York: Harper & Brothers, 1960.

Hofstadter, Richard, and Wilson Smith, eds., *American Higher Education; A Documentary History*. Chicago: University of Chicago Press, 1961.

Jacob, Philip E., *Changing Values in College; An Exploratory Study of the Impact of College Teaching*. New York: Harper & Brothers, 1957.

Keezer, Dexter M., *Financing Higher Education: 1960–1970*. New York: McGraw-Hill Book Co., Inc., 1959.

Kentucky Legislative Research Commission, *State Support for Municipal Colleges*. Frankfort: 1958.

Langsam, Walter C., *Report of the President for the Academic Years 1959–60, 1960–61*. Cincinnati: The University of Cincinnati, 1962.

Ligon, Ernest M., *Dimensions of Character*. New York: The Macmillan Co., 1956.

McConnell, T. R., *A General Pattern for American Public Higher Education*. The Carnegie Series in American Education. New York: McGraw-Hill Book Co., Inc., 1962.

Mayer, Frederick, *New Directions for the American University*. Washington, D.C.: Public Affairs Press, 1957.

Millett, John D., *Higher Education in Ohio: 1962*. Report by the Chairman, Ohio Interim Commission on Education Beyond the High School. [Oxford, Ohio: 1962]

National Conference on Higher Education, *Current Issues in Higher Education, 1961*. Washington, D.C.: Association for Higher Education, 1961.

National Education Association of the United States, *Salaries Paid and Salary Practices in Universities, Colleges, and Junior Colleges, 1961–1962*. Higher Education Series Research Report 1961–62. Washington, D.C.: NEA Research Division, February 1962.

——, *Teacher Supply and Demand*. Higher Education Series Research Report 1961–1962. Washington, D.C.: NEA Research Division, 1962.

Ness, Frederic W., ed., *A Regional Faculty Orientation Program*. Washington, D.C.: Association of American Colleges, 1961.

*Operation and Financing of State Programs*. State of Ohio, Michael V. DiSalle, Governor. Columbus, Ohio: 1962.

Orleans, Jacob S., *Teacher Education Enrollment Needs of the Four Municipal Colleges of New York City*. New York: Office of Research and Evaluation, Division of Teacher Education, College of The City of New York, 1953.

Petersen, Renee and William Petersen, *University Adult Education; A Guide to Policy*. New York: Harper & Brothers, 1950.

Rogers, Francis M., *Higher Education in the United States; A Summary View*, 3rd ed. rev. Cambridge: Harvard University Press, 1960.

Schoenfeld, Clarence A., *The University and Its Publics*. New York: Harper & Brothers, 1954.

Selden, William K., *Accreditation: A Struggle Over Standards in Higher Education*. New York: Harper & Brothers, 1960.

Shuster, George N., *Education and Moral Wisdom*. New York: Harper & Brothers, 1960.

Smith, Huston, *Purposes of Higher Education*. New York: Harper & Brothers, 1955.

Tead, Ordway, *Character Building and Higher Education*. New York: The Macmillan Co., 1953.

Truscot, Bruce (pseud.), *Red Brick University*. Harmondsworth, Middlesex: Pelican Books, Ltd., 1951.

U.S. President's Committee on Education Beyond the High School, *Edu-*

*cation Beyond the High School: Needs and Resources.* Washington, D.C.: Government Printing Office, 1957.

——, *First Interim Report to the President,* Washington, D.C.: Government Printing Office, 1956.

Washburn University of Topeka, *Statutes, By-laws and Supplementary Retirement Program.* Topeka: The University, 1953.

Weatherford, Willis D., ed., *Goals of Higher Education.* Cambridge: Harvard University Press, 1960.

Weinstock, Ruth, *Space and Dollars: An Urban University Expands.* New York: Educational Facilities Laboratories, 1961.

West, Leonard J., *College and the Years After: A Career Study of Municipal College Graduates.* New York: Board of Higher Education, College of the City of New York, 1952.

Western College Association, *Addresses: Effective Utilization of Faculty Resources in a Period of Rapidly Expanding Enrollments.* Fresno, Calif.: The Association, 1956.

*Index*

# Index

## A

Academic freedom:
  in budget and curriculum, 16–17
  study by MacIver, 12
Admissions:
  recruiting, 66
  requirements, 66, 68
  selectivity, 9, 79, 82
Adult education:
  Association of Urban Universities report, 85
  evening classes, 85
  executive development, 85, 86
  special interest courses, 86
Alumni:
  as source of professional manpower, 41
  as source of support, 21–22
Aristotle, 13
Association of Urban Universities:
  adult education report, 85
  enrollment study, 7
  future of municipal universities (1914), 97
  on multiple employment of faculty, 54
  newsletters, 46, 76
  reports of annual meetings, 54, 65, 72, 97

## B

Benton, William, 88
Blade, The (Toledo), 77
Brooklyn College enrollment, 3

## C

Canham, Erwin, 28
Carnegie Foundation for Advancement of Teaching, 82
Charleston, S.C., The College of, 4
Citizenship, 80, 81
City College (N.Y.) enrollment, 3
City officials, 42, 44
City University of New York:
  enrollment, 3
  state financial support, 18, 19
  student fees, 18

Clientele of a university, 17
Columbia University, 31, 32
Commission on Financing Higher Education, 67
Committee on Education Beyond the High School, 78
Community affairs, participation in:
  joint purchasing, 43
  physical planning, 43
  zoning, 43
Community colleges:
  financial support, 2
  general education, 80, 81
  governing boards, 2
  guidance into, 83
  public acceptance, 83
  public support, 83, 98
  purposes, 77
  technical education, 30, 80–81
Conant, James, 27
Cooperation, inter-institutional, 31–32
Cooperative education, University of Cincinnati, 38, 64
Cosmopolitanism, 26–29, 33, 35
Council of State Governments, 13
Criticism of colleges, 88

## D

Dartmouth College case, 12
Definition of municipal university, 1–2
DeKiewiet, Cornelis W., 36
Delo, David M., 54
DeVane, Wm. C., 52, 56
Diekhoff, John S., 1, 99
Directors, Board of (see Governing Boards)
Dodds, Harold W., 50
Drop-outs, 83–84

## E

Educational Record, The, 36
Education Directory, 1961–62, 2
Education News, 89, 92
Endowments, 20
Enrollments:
  diversity, 76–77
  future increases, 14, 78–79
  increase since 1900, 66–67
  1961 statistics, 3

Entrance requirements (*see* Admissions)

Evening classes (*see* Adult education)

**F**

Faculty:
cultural opportunities, 52
doctoral degrees, 53–54
outside employment, 54
quality, 57
responsibilities, 55–56
salaries, 54
status, 59
talent, 31–32, 56–57
Fees (*see also* Tuition):
resident and non-resident, 21, 67
three-level, 67
Financial support:
allocations, 18
alumni, 21–22
appropriations, 18, 42
endowments, 20
future, 97–99
gifts, 22
local taxation, 2, 17–19
research, sponsored, 22
state:
City University of New York, 4
Midwestern University of Wichita Falls, 4
Newark College of Engineering, 3
Ohio's municipal universities, 6
University of Louisville, 3, 19
Wayne University, 4
student fees, 17–18, 20
Former municipally-supported institutions, 4

**G**

General education, 30–31, 80–82
Gould, Samuel B., 46
Governing Boards:
meetings, 1, 90, 95
membership, 2
selection, 1–2
term, 2
Graduate programs, 39

**H**

Haack, Arno J., 65
Harbison, Winfred A., 16
Heald, Henry T., 7
Henry, David D., 76

History of municipal universities, 5, 6, 16
Hoover, Robert C., 35
Hunter College, enrollment, 3

**I**

Income (*see* Financial support)
Industry, benefits from:
faculty source, 39
research sponsorship, 38–39
student experience, 38

**J**

Junior colleges (*see* Community Colleges)

**K**

Klotsche, J. Martin, 32

**L**

Langsam, Walter C., v–vi, 38
Leadership training, 37

**M**

MacIver, Robert M., 12
Mason, Robert D., 41
Medical education, 30
Medical schools:
University of Cincinnati, 19–20
University of Louisville, 19–20
Michigan State University, 7
Mill, John Stuart, 45
Murlin, Lemuel H., 97

**N**

National Defense Education Act, 71
Newark College of Engineering:
local tax support, 17–18
state support, 3, 19
student fees, 18
Newman, Cardinal John Henry, 27
News (*see also* Publicity):
defining, 89
education, 89, 92
financial, 91
open door policy, 90
sports, 89, 95
News media, training for, 91
Newspaper:
readers, 91

Newspaper (*cont.*)
  reporters, 89
  student, 90, 93
New York City Board of Higher Education:
  appropriations, 18
  membership, 2
  responsibilities, 3
New York University, 32
Northwestern University, 32

O

Ohio, higher education in:
  enrollment, 6–7
  private institutions, 6
  tax-supported institutions, 6
Ohio municipal universities (*see* University of Akron; University of Cincinnati; University of Toledo)
Ohio Northern University, 31
Ohio State University, The, 7
Opportunity, equality of, 33–34

P

Parker, Garland C., 3
Patrons of a university, 16–17
Press, the:
  criticism by, 89, 92, 95
  criticism of, 92, 94
  educational value of, 92
  responsibility of, 96
Pressure groups, 16–17
Private colleges:
  admission, 79
  state support, 8
Professional education, 10, 30
Public higher education:
  necessity, 14
  significance, 13
Public relations:
  of the Board, 24
  of the President, 24
  with the press, 88
  with the taxpayers, 23–24
Public school relationships, 39–40
Public service, education for, 43–45
Publicity (*see also* News):
  athletic, 95
  benefits, 91–93
  board meetings, 90, 94
  education news, 89–90, 92
  financial, 90
  student newspaper, 90, 93

Q

Queens College, enrollment, 3

R

Radio, 94–95
Recruiting, 66
Reinert, Paul C., 55
Religion:
  courses, 73–75
  influence on choice of college, 72
  Judeo-Christian tradition, 73
  neglect in public institutions, 73–74
Research:
  importance, 46
  public responsibility, 13–14, 50–51
  support, 13–14, 47, 50
  types, 46, 48–49
Robinson, Frederick B., 85
Role of higher education, 4, 5, 8–10, 14–15, 34, 87

S

Salaries, faculty, 54
Schoenfeld, Clarence A., 88
Scholarships, grants-in-aid, and loans, 71
Sevaried, Eric, 89
Spathelf, Victor F., 71–72
State financial support:
  for municipal universities, 3–4, 6, 19
  for private institutions, 8
  for special programs, 19
Students:
  church influence on, 72
  motivation toward college, 67–71, 84
  newspaper, 90, 93
  organization, 63–64
  resident and non-resident, 5–6, 21, 63–64
  school spirit, 63, 65
  social needs, 26, 28
  work opportunities, 38, 71
  work schedules, 64
Student Union, 64
Syracuse University, 31

T

Teacher (*see also* Faculty):
  education, 4, 39–40
  shortage, 57–58
  supply, 58–60, 82

Technical Education (*see* Community colleges)
Television, 58, 94–95
Traffic, campus, 64–65
Transportation, 5–6, 64–65
Truscot, Bruce, 50
Trustees (*see* Governing Boards)
Tuition sources, 70–71 (*see also* Fees)
Two-year programs (*see* Community colleges)

U

University of Akron, The:
  enrollment, 3, 6
  local tax support, 17–18
  student fees, 18
University of Buffalo, 8, 31
University of California, 57
University of Chicago, 32
University of Cincinnati:
  cooperative education, 38
  enrollment, 3, 6
  financial support:
    endowment, 20
    local tax, 17
    research grants, gifts, etc., 20
    state support of vocational education, 19
    suburban, 20
    student fees, 18
    tax millage, 18
University of Detroit, 8
University of Houston, 8
University of Louisville:
  enrollment, 3
  financial support:
    county-wide, 19
    endowment, 20
    local tax, 17
    research grants, gifts, etc., 20
    state, 3, 19
    student fees, 18
University of Michigan, 7

University of Omaha, Municipal:
  enrollment, 3
  financial support:
    local tax, 18–19
    state, 19
    student fees, 18
University of Rochester, 31
University of Toledo, The:
  alumni seminar, 60
  business alumni study, 41
  engineering college, 31
  enrollment, 3, 6
  financial support:
    local tax, 18, 22
    state, 19
    student fees, 18
  public school relationships, 39–41
University of Wichita:
  enrollment, 3
  financial support:
    local tax, 17, 19
    state, 19
    student fees, 18
Urbanization, 8, 37

V

Van Houten, Robert W., 4
Veterans, 64, 67

W

Washburn University of Topeka:
  enrollment, 3
  financial support:
    endowment, 20
    local tax, 17, 19
    state, 19
    student fees, 18
Wayne State University, 8, 99
Weinstock, Ruth, 62
Wells, Donald E., 72
Wilbern, York, 45
Woods, Donald Z., 87

X

Xavier University, 8